The
Golden
Retriever

An Owner's Guide To

A HAPPY HEALTHY PET

Howell Book House

Howell Book House
A Simon & Schuster Macmillan Company
1633 Broadway
New York, NY 10019

Library of Congress Cataloging-in-Publication Data
Cairns, Julie.
The Golden Retriever: an owner's guide to a happy, healthy pet/ by Julie Cairns.
    p. cm.
Includes bibliographical references.

ISBN: 0-87605-380-0

1. Golden retrievers. I. Title.
SF429.G63C35   1995
636.7'52–dc20   95-15668
      CIP

Manufactured in the United States of America
10 9 8 7 6 5 4 3 2

Series Director: Dominique De Vito
Series Assistant Director: Felice Primeau
Book Design: Michele Laseau
Cover Design: Iris Jeromnimon
Illustration: Jeff Yesh
Photography:
    Cover by Kerrin Winter & Dale Churchill; puppy by Pets by Paulette
    Courtesy of the AKC: 15, 18, 20
    Joan Balzarini: 96
    Mary Bloom: 33, 87, 96, 136, 145
    Paulette Braun/Pets by Paulette: 5, 9, 11, 25, 32, 38, 40, 41, 44, 55, 96
    Buckinghamhill American Cocker Spaniels: 148
    Sian Cox: 134
    Dr. Ian Dunbar: 98, 101, 103, 111, 116–117, 122, 123, 127
    Dan Lyons: 96
    Cathy Merrithew: 129
    Liz Palika: 133
    Janice Raines: 132
    Susan Rezy: 2–3, 30, 31, 36-37, 57, 62, 71, 72, 77, 96–97
    Judith Strom: 17, 22, 24, 27, 43, 45, 47, 51, 52, 60, 96, 107, 110, 128, 130, 135, 137, 139, 140, 144, 149, 150
    Kerrin Winter & Dale Churchill: 7, 8, 12, 21, 29, 56, 59
Production Team: Troy Barnes, John Carroll, Jama Carter, Kathleen Caulfield, Trudy Coler, Vic Peterson, Terri Sheehan, Marvin Van Tiem, Amy DeAngelis and Kathy Iwasaki

Contents

Welcome
to the
World
of the

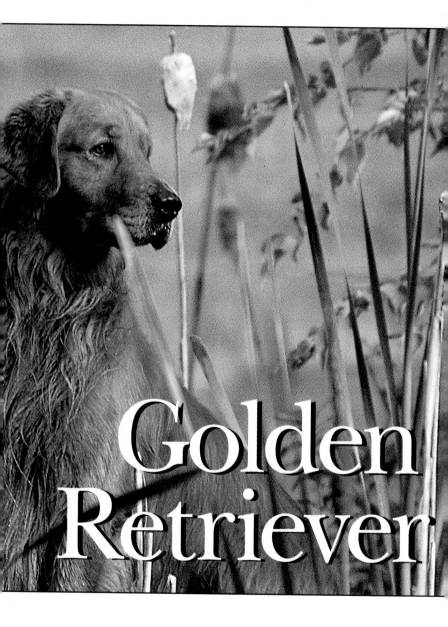

part one

Golden Retriever

External Features of the Golden Retriever

Muzzle

Stop

Skull

Cheek

Crest

Neck

Shoulder

Withers

Wrist

Forearm

Elbow

Pastern

Dewclaw

Back

Loin

Stifle or Knee

Croup

Toes

Hock

chapter 1

What
is a
Golden Retriever?

The overall appearance of the Golden Retriever is described in the opening paragraph of the breed's official American Kennel Club "breed standard," which was revised and adopted in 1982. The Golden should be an athletic dog, whose overall attitude is as much a part of its "being" as any physical components. It is important to keep in mind when reading the standard and trying to match one's own Golden to it

that the standard describes an *ideal* Golden, and some sections are geared toward a show interpretation. A dog may be a very good specimen of the breed and still not be of current show quality or type. Likewise, some dogs with faults often do well in the breed ring. The key is in understanding what the standard is trying to describe and being objective in measuring one's own dog against it.

General Appearance—A symmetrical, powerful, active dog, sound and well put together, not clumsy nor long in the leg, displaying a kindly expression and possessing a personality that is eager, alert and self-confident. Primarily a hunting dog, he should be shown in hard working condition. Overall appearance, balance, gait and purpose to be given more emphasis than any of his component parts.

Size—Males 23–24 inches in height at the withers; females 21½–22½ inches. Dogs up to one inch above or below standard should be proportionately penalized. Deviation in height of more than one inch from the standard shall disqualify. Length from breastbone to point of buttocks slightly greater than height at withers in ratio of 12:11. Weight for dogs 65–75 pounds; bitches 55–65 pounds.

WHAT IS A BREED STANDARD?

A breed standard—a detailed description of an individual breed—is meant to portray the *ideal* specimen of that breed. This includes ideal structure, temperament, gait, type—all aspects of the dog. Because the standard describes an ideal specimen, it isn't based on any particular dog. It is a concept against which judges compare actual dogs and breeders strive to produce dogs. At a dog show, the dog that wins is the one that comes closest, in the judge's opinion, to the standard for its breed. Breed standards are written by the breed parent clubs, the national organizations formed to oversee the well-being of the breed. They are voted on and approved by the members of the parent clubs.

Measuring Height

The standard Golden is a medium-sized dog. Measuring a dog's height is done by using a yardstick and a flat surface (for example, a sheet of cardboard) that is gently placed at the flat area where the neck and back meet (the withers; see illustration of the parts of the body). Be careful that the angle of the flat surface to the yardstick is perpendicular, or it may be off by an inch or more. A Golden's height may vary an inch over or under and remain within the standard. This means that a male can be between 20 and 25 inches and a female from 20½ to 23½ and be within the standard height. The Golden should be slightly longer in body than tall. The weight recommendations are meant for dogs of proper height that are in working condition. Obviously, an overweight dog, or one suffering from poor nutrition, will not fall within these weights. The tendency for Goldens to be larger (taller and heavier) than the standard allows is due to certain trends over the years; a moderate-sized Golden is more suitable for the various jobs it performs and will be subject to fewer soundness problems.

Head—Broad in skull, slightly arches laterally and longitudinally without prominence of frontal bones (forehead) or occipital bones. Stop well defined but not abrupt. Foreface deep and wide, nearly as long as skull. Muzzle straight in profile, blending smoothly and strongly into skull; when viewed in profile or from above, slightly deeper and wider at stop than at tip. No heaviness in flews. Removal of whiskers is permitted but not preferred.

The head's proportion and expression define the Golden Retriever.

While the head does not affect overall soundness, the way a dog works or its ability to be a good pet, it is the way the head is proportioned and the facial expressions that define the Golden Retriever. A narrow skull with a prominent occiput (a point at the back end of the head) is as unattractive in a dog as an overly broad, coarse head. The stop is the area between the eyes from the top of the head to the beginning of the muzzle (nose). There should be a definite difference in these two planes. A dog with no stop has only a slope from the head to muzzle as opposed to an angle that indicates depth. The muzzle should taper slightly to the tip of the nose, but it should not be pointed. A common fault in Goldens is a Roman nose. In profile this appears as a pronounced hump on the top of the muzzle. The skin on the sides of the muzzle (the flews) should fit tightly against the mouth as opposed to hanging loosely below the jaws.

Eyes—Friendly and intelligent in expression, medium large with dark, close-fitting rims, set well apart and reasonably deep in the sockets. Color preferably dark brown, medium brown acceptable, slant eyes and narrow, triangular eyes detract from correct expression and are to be faulted. No white or haw visible when looking straight ahead. Dogs showing evidence of functional abnormality of eyelids or eyelashes (such as, but not limited to, trichiasis, entropian, ectropian, or distichiasis) are to be excused from the ring.

Here's Looking at You

The eyes are the single most important physical characteristic of the Golden. The eyes mirror the dog's personality and character, which are what make a Golden what it is—intelligent, trusting and fun-loving. Light eyes lack expression and often give a dog a harsh appearance, which is totally atypical of a Golden. Slanted or almond-shaped eyes are not correct, nor are eyes that are too round and large or eyes that protrude. A lid that hangs loosely around the eye makes it easier for foreign objects, such as grass seeds, to get into the eye. The eye abnormalities mentioned above need to be diagnosed by a veterinarian. Dogs afflicted with some of these conditions should not be bred.

The eyes mirror the dog's personality.

Teeth—Scissors bite, in which the outer side of the lower incisors touches the inner side of the upper incisors. Undershot or overshot is a disqualification. Misalignment of teeth (irregular placement of incisors) or a level bite (incisors meet each other edge to edge) is undesirable, but not to be confused with overshot or undershot. Full dentition. Obvious gaps are serious faults.

The undershot dog's teeth on the lower jaw protrude beyond its upper-jaw teeth. In the overshot jaw, the upper teeth jut significantly beyond the lower teeth. Another common mouth problem is the wry bite, where the teeth of the upper and lower jaws are offset and do not meet normally when upper and lower teeth meet. Premolars are the teeth usually missing in Goldens, though sometimes molars are, too.

Nose—Black or brownish black, though fading to lighter shade in cold weather not serious. Pink nose or one seriously lacking in pigmentation to be faulted.

Ears—Rather short with front edge attached well behind and just above the eye and falling close to the cheek. When pulled forward, tips of ears should just cover the eyes. Low, hound-like ear set to be faulted.

Correctly sized and placed ears are an important component to the overall look of the Golden. The standard mentions hound-like ears but does not mention the equally unattractive alternative. This is the dog whose ears are set too high, especially if those ears are abnormally small.

Goldens are popular assistance dogs.

Neck—Medium long, merging gradually into well laid back shoulders, giving sturdy, muscular appearance. Untrimmed natural ruff. No throatiness.

Body—Well balanced, short coupled, deep through the chest. Chest between forelegs at least as wide as a man's closed hand including thumb, with well developed forechest. Brisket extends to elbow. Ribs long and well sprung but not barrel shaped, extending well towards hindquarters. Loin short, muscular, wide and deep, with very little tuck-up. Back line strong and level from withers to slightly sloping croup, whether standing or moving. Slabsidedness, narrow chest, lack of depth in brisket, sloping backline, roach or sway back, excessive tuck-up, flat or steep croup to be faulted.

Forequarters—Muscular, well coordinated with hindquarters and capable of free movement. Shoulder blades long and well laid back with upper tips fairly close together at withers. Upper arms appear about the same length as the blades, setting the elbows back beneath the upper tip of the blades, close to the ribs without looseness. Legs, viewed from the front, straight with good bone, but not to the point of coarseness. Pasterns short and strong, sloping slightly with no suggestion of weakness.

Hindquarters—Broad and strongly muscled. Profile of croup slopes slightly; the pelvic bone slopes at a slightly greater angle (approximately 30 degrees from horizontal). In a natural stance, the femur joins the pelvis at approximately a 90 degree angle; stifles well bent; hocks well let down with short, strong rear pasterns. Legs straight when viewed from rear. Cow hocks, spread hocks, and sickle hocks to be faulted.

THE AMERICAN KENNEL CLUB

Familiarly referred to as "the AKC," the American Kennel Club is a nonprofit organization devoted to the advancement of purebred dogs. The AKC maintains a registry of recognized breeds and adopts and enforces rules for dog events including shows, obedience trials, field trials, hunting tests, lure coursing, herding, earthdog trials, agility and the Canine Good Citizen program. It is a club of clubs, established in 1884 and composed, today, of over 500 autonomous dog clubs throughout the United States. Each club is represented by a delegate; the delegates make up the legislative body of the AKC, voting on rules and electing directors. The American Kennel Club maintains the Stud Book, the record of every dog ever registered with the AKC, and publishes a variety of materials on purebred dogs, including a monthly magazine, books and numerous educational pamphlets. For more information, contact the AKC at the address listed in Chapter 13, "Resources" and look for the names of their publications in Chapter 12, "Recommended Reading."

A Sporty Physique

The description of the manner in which a Golden body should be put together is meant for utilitarian purposes. A sporting dog must have correct structure to perform its job properly. Even if our dog's sole purpose is to be a companion, a correctly structured body will help ensure the active life a Golden relishes. In practical working terms the strength and power described in the strong neck, broad front, straight legs and correct angles is required for a dog that might spend the day in the field hunting and carrying birds through cover.

Feet—Medium size, round, compact, and well knuckled, with thick pads. Excess hair may be trimmed to show natural size and contour. Dewclaws on forelegs may be removed but are normally left on. Splayed or hare feet to be faulted.

Again, the foot structure described is best for an active, working dog. The faulty hare or splayed foot is one that is pointed in structure as opposed to round. The toes are spread out and the foot itself looks flattened (splayed). Feet like these do not stand up to exercise, and the dog's entire body will eventually suffer.

Tail—Well set on, thick and muscular at the base, following the natural line of the croup. Tail bones extend to, but not below, the point of hock. Carried with merry action, level or with moderate upward curve; never curled over back or between legs.

A whole family of Goldens!

The tail is another physical part of the dog that speaks for its personality. "Carried with merry action" may be interpreted as wagging almost all of the time. A "gay" tail, one that is carried above the level of the back, is not only an improper tail set, but it may also be indicative of an aggressive temperament. Similarly, the Golden that carries its tail low or tucked between its rear legs may be spooky or shy—equally incorrect Golden behaviors.

Coat—Dense and water repellent with good undercoat. Outer coat firm and resilient, neither coarse nor silky, lying close to the body; may be straight or wavy. Moderate feathering on back of forelegs and on underbody; heavier feathering on front of neck, back of thighs and underside of tail. Coat on head, paws, and front of legs is short and even. Excessive length, open coats and limp, soft coats are very undesirable. Feet may be trimmed and stray hairs neatened, but the natural appearance of coat or outline should not be altered by cutting or clipping.

The Golden has a dense, lustrous coat.

The correct Golden coat as described by the standard is necessary for a hunting dog that is used on land and water. The coat should act as a protection to the rough cover that a dog might encounter. Due to its length and feathers, a Golden's coat will pick up burrs that would never be found on a Labrador Retriever or Chesapeake Bay Retriever. A coat of moderate length is desirable, but excessively heavy coats with long feathers are useless for a working dog. Many hunters choose to trim their Golden's feathers during hunting season, but on a properly coated Golden it should not be much of a problem. The coat should act as a repellent to water, rather than soaking it up like a sponge. A Golden with a proper coat will come out of the water, shake a couple of times and be nearly dry. If the Golden coat is wavy, these waves are usually on the hair along the back. Occasionally one sees a truly curly Golden, with curls all over the body. The hair on the legs, face and feathers is straight. This is no doubt a throwback to the Tweed Water Spaniel that was used in the original crosses during the initial development of the breed.

Color—Rich, lustrous golden of various shades. Feathering may be lighter than the rest of the body.

With exception of graying or lightening of face or body due to age, any white marking, other than a few white hairs on the chest, should be penalized according to its extent. Allowable light shadings are not to be confused with white markings. Predominant body color which is either extremely pale or extremely dark is undesirable. Some latitude should be given to the light puppy whose coloring shows promise of deepening with maturity. Any noticeable area of black or other off-color is a serious fault.

How Golden Is Golden?

No other feature of the Golden receives more comment than color. A wide range of colors is permissible, from light to dark golden. It is really a personal preference. Originally most Goldens were darker gold, but during the last twenty years a light golden color has become more popular. The presence of white markings on the body is the fault most easily noticed by the novice. White often appears on the chest, but also appears on other areas of the body, such as the top of the head, muzzle and the feet. White markings anywhere other than the chest are not desirable, but they will in no way affect a dog as a pet or working dog.

Gait—When trotting, gait is free, smooth, powerful, and well coordinated, showing good reach. Viewed from any position, legs turn neither in nor out, nor do feet cross or interfere with each other. As speed increases, feet tend to converge toward line of balance. It is recommended that dogs be shown on a loose lead to reflect true gait.

This describes the correct movement of a properly structured dog. If a dog moves poorly or inefficiently it will tire more easily. The description above is how dogs are viewed in the show ring.

Temperament—Friendly, reliable and trustworthy. Quarrelsomeness or hostility toward other dogs or people in normal situations, or an unwarranted show of timidity or nervousness, is not in keeping with Golden Retriever character. Such actions should be penalized according to their significance.

13

In the breed ring a judge has very little time to assess a dog's personality. A Golden owner reading this standard has a better knowledge of his dog's temperament, though we may not be certain of how our dog will react to other dogs in stressful environments. A Golden with a good temperament is stable and reacts predictably in any normal situation.

Faults—Any departure from the described ideal should be considered faulty to the degree it interferes with the breed's purpose or is contrary to breed character.

Disqualifications—1. Deviation in height of more than one inch from standard either way. 2. Undershot or overshot bite.

There is no perfect Golden in the world; almost every dog has some fault or weakness. It is the *overall* appearance and attitude that is most important in evaluating the Golden. There are many faults and a few disqualifications in the Golden Retriever standard, and while they might affect a dog if it were to be entered in a dog show, they will have no bearing on a dog's ability to be a good companion. Remember this when reading the standard and when applying it to your own dog.

chapter 2

The
Golden Retriever's
Ancestry

Retrievers became increasingly popular in Britain in the 1800s with the growth of the sport of bird hunting. Retrievers were considered the elite of the sporting breeds, as they were so versatile and could be used for waterfowl and upland game. There were many crosses of breeds used during this time, and there is no doubt that several retrievers existed prior to the actual development

of the Golden as we know it today that were very Golden-like in appearance. It is Sir Dudley Majoribanks, later Lord Tweedmouth, who is credited with the actual creation of the Golden Retriever due to his breeding program in Scotland in the mid- to late 1800s. All modern-day Goldens can trace their origins to Lord Tweedmouth's breedings.

Lord Tweedmouth acquired a young male yellow Wavy (Flat) Coated Retriever in 1866. The yellow color is recessive, and to this day occurs occasionally in the Flat Coat Retriever breed. Existing photos of this dog, who was named Nous, show a large, wavy-coated dog that looked very much like a Golden Retriever. Also acquired was a Tweed Water Spaniel bitch named Belle, a member of another popular hunting breed of the region. These dogs were known for their swimming ability, superior intelligence and wonderful temperaments. They were medium in size, liver colored (any shade of yellow to brown) and had a tightly curled coat with very little feathering. When one considers that all retriever breeds share a similar genetic base, and that the major difference in the Golden's development from the others is the Tweed Water Spaniel, it is understandable how some of the traits that make the Golden unique from other retriever breeds are derived.

Early Breeding

The breeding of Nous and Belle in 1868 resulted in four yellow puppies: Ada, Crocus, Cowslip and Primrose. Cowslip was retained by Lord Tweedmouth for his planned breeding program. She was subsequently bred to Tweed, another Tweed Water Spaniel, and later to Sampson, a Red Setter. The later breeding is thought to have been done to enhance the nose and to fix color. In 1884 a second yellow Nous was whelped. This dog's sire was Jack, a son of Sampson and Cowslip. His dam was Zoe,

WHERE DID DOGS COME FROM?

It can be argued that dogs were right there at man's side from the beginning of time. As soon as human beings began to document their existence, the dog was among their drawings and inscriptions. Dogs were not just friends, they served a purpose: There were dogs to hunt birds, pull sleds, herd sheep, burrow after rats—even sit in laps! What your dog was originally bred to do influences the way it behaves. The American Kennel Club recognizes over 140 breeds, and there are hundreds more distinct breeds around the world. To make sense of the breeds, they are grouped according to their size or function. The AKC has seven groups:

1) Sporting, 2) Working,
3) Herding, 4) Hounds,
5) Terriers, 6) Toys,
7) Nonsporting

Can you name a breed from each group? Here's some help: (1) Golden Retriever; (2) Doberman Pinscher; (3) Collie; (4) Beagle; (5) Scottish Terrier; (6) Maltese; and (7) Dalmatian. All modern domestic dogs (Canis familiaris) are related, however different they look, and are all descended from Canis lupus, the gray wolf.

whose sire was a black Wavy Coat and whose dam was Topsy, a daughter of Tweed and Cowslip. The final pedigree entered in Lord Tweedmouth's stud book is the breeding of the second Nous to Queenie. Queenie was the daughter of a black Wavy (Flat) Coat and Gill, a littermate to the second Nous.

Two yellow puppies resulted from this breeding, Prim and Rose. These two are the link of the modern Golden with Lord Tweedmouth's original dogs. During this time there were other sportsmen who had obtained dogs from Lord Tweedmouth and no doubt bred Golden-type dogs, but none kept the detailed records to document any formal breeding program.

The Golden has always been a sportsman's dog.

In England, the first Goldens were registered by the Kennel Club in 1904 and were listed along with Wavy or Flat Coats. After 1913 they were separated by color and known as Golden or Yellow Retrievers. The official term, "Golden Retriever," was not recognized until 1920. Goldens made their first appearance in field trials in the early 1900s and achieved some success. At the same time they began to be entered in dog shows. One of the most important early breeders was Lord Harcourt, who used the Culham prefix on his dogs. His foundation pair, Culham Brass and Culham Rossa, were descendants of Prim and Rose. A grandson of these two, Champion (Ch.) Noranby Campfire, born in 1913, was the first dog to finish a bench championship. Mrs. Charlesworth owned this dog and was a driving force in the breed until the 1950s. Her dogs were all registered with the Noranby kennel name.

The two world wars were a serious deterrent to the growth of the breed. During these times breeding almost came to a halt, and dog activities ceased. During World War II some breeders sent their dogs to the United States for safety. After both wars there was a serious drop in quality, as nearly anything that looked like a Golden Retriever was bred to supply demand. An interest in lighter-colored dogs began in the 1930s. Prior to this, most Goldens were relatively dark in color. Eventually the breed standard was changed to allow for light- or cream-colored dogs. This would have an eventual impact on how Goldens would look worldwide.

A Golden Retriever from generations past.

Getting to the USA

Goldens appeared in the United States as early as the 1890s. There are photographs of Lord Tweedmouth's son, the Hon. Archie Majoribanks, at his ranch in Texas with a Golden Retriever named Lady. Lady was a descendant of Lord Tweedmouth's dogs and was also supposedly the grandam of Lord Harcourt's Culham Brass. There are other reports of Goldens throughout Canada and the United States in the early 1900s, but none of them were ever registered.

The breed would not make an official entry into the United States until the 1920s. This was an era when Americans were enamored of anything British, including their sporting dogs. Along with Labrador Retrievers, a few Goldens were imported by some of America's wealthiest and most prominent citizens.

Robert Appleton, a resident of East Hampton, Long Island, and the retired head of a publishing company, was the first to actually register a Golden Retriever with the American Kennel Club in 1925. This was an imported three-year-old male named Lomberdale Blondin. He also imported and registered a female, Dan Hill Judy. These two produced the first registered litter in December 1925.

During these early years Goldens were registered and shown along with Labrador Retrievers. They did not gain recognition as a separate breed until 1932. During this time as the handful of fanciers grew, some dogs were shown sporadically, and there was an occasional litter of puppies. However, none of these dogs would go on to have any influence on the breed as it grew. The first truly serious Golden breeder in the United States was Dr. Charles Large of New York City. Beginning in 1931 he imported a number of dogs that were shown and became the basis of his breeding program. He used the kennel name Fernova and was an early activist in the attempt to form a national breed club. His efforts were never realized, because he died in 1933. Most of his dogs were acquired by Michael Clemens, who continued Dr. Large's breedings using the kennel name Frantelle for his dogs.

Goldens of this era that found their way to the estates of the wealthy were acquired not only out of curiosity but also for use as hunting dogs. Few actually made it into homes or lived as pets. They were usually in large kennel facilities overseen by the kennel managers. It is interesting to note that a Golden was entered in the first AKC Licensed Retriever Field Trial held on Long Island in 1931. This young imported female went on to become Ch. Lady Burns and was one of two entered in the Puppy Stake.

The Golden Retriever finally received the boost it needed when Col. Samuel Magoffin of Vancouver, British Columbia, imported a young male from England named Speedwell Pluto in 1932. Pluto was a champion in both the United States and Canada. He was the first Golden to win a Best in Show Award and was a successful hunting dog as well. He is considered to be the foundation sire of the breed in America. Col. Magoffin's Rockhaven Kennels were based in Vancouver. He also founded Gilnockie Kennels, located in Englewood, Colorado. He imported a number of dogs from England that would be influential in the development of the Golden breed. Col. Magoffin had relatives in Minnesota and Wisconsin who followed suit in obtaining Goldens. Ralph Boalt of Winona, Minnesota, at this time was Magoffin's brother-in-law. He imported a bitch from England named Patience of Yelme, who would become the beginning of Stilrovin Kennels. However, Stilrovin is most famous for Gilnockie Coquette from Col. Magoffin's kennel in Colorado. By two different sires she produced three field champions, a dual champion and a bench champion. These dogs would be among the most influential producers as the breed developed in the late 1940s and 1950s. Ralph Boalt continued to breed Goldens that were successful in field trials through the 1960s. At about the same time Ralph's brother, Ben Boalt, started Beavertail Kennels (later changed to Gunnerman) in Wisconsin. His original dogs were all of Rockhaven breeding.

Midwestern Goldens

Another early Golden fancier in Minnesota was Henry Christian, who started Goldwood Kennels in 1933. He imported Sprite of Aldgrove from England and a Ch.

A 1962 Best in Show winner, Ch. Cragmount's Peter.

Speedwell Pluto son, Rockhaven Rory, from Canada. Both would complete their championships. Rory was one of the most widely used stud dogs among breeders in the area. Goldwood Kennels produced FC Goldwood Tuck and two of the first great Golden obedience competitors, Goldwood Michael UD and Goldwood Toby UD. The latter was the first Golden to earn a Utility Degree.

The St. Louis, Missouri, area was another region of early Golden activity. Mr. and Mrs. Mahlon Wallace, Jr., and John K. Wallace began importing from England in 1933. The breeding of two of their imports, Speedwell Reuben and Ch. Speedwell Tango, resulted in FC Rip.

In 1939 he was the first Golden to complete a field championship. His record of consistency and points earned in Open Stakes holds up even today as one of the best among Goldens. Also noteworthy is the fact that he was owner-amateur–handled in an era when almost all dogs in field trials were run by professionals. John K. Wallace used the kennel name Whitebridge on his dogs. An important import of his was Eng.-Am. Ch. Bingo of Yelme. Bingo was a successful field trial competitor as well as a champion. He is best remembered as the sire of Ralph Boalt's great outstanding producer, Gilnockie Coquette. When the war began in Europe a large number of the dogs of England's Yelme Kennels went to John K. Wallace. Many of these dogs did well in American field trials and were successful producers of working dogs.

Another early English import whose influence must be mentioned is Eng. Ch. Marine of Woolley. He was imported and owned by Blue Leader Kennels of Santa Barbara, California, and was one of the first Goldens in that section of the country.

Goldens are active field trial competitors.

Marine is important as he sired littermates Rockhaven Ben Bolt and Rockhaven Judy, both imported to Minnesota from Canada. Ben Bolt was owned by Ralph Boalt, was run in field trials and was an influential sire of the breed in the late 1930s and 1940s in the area. Judy was one of the foundation dams of Woodend Kennels. She produced several top field dogs that would become important as the Golden gained popularity as a field competitor. Woodend Kennels is also notable as having bred NFC King Midas of Woodend. In 1941 he was the first National Field Champion.

The growth and popularity of the Golden in the midwest in these years was a remarkable phenomenon.

This was an era when hunting upland game and waterfowl was enjoying its peak in popularity among a growing number of hunters, and the midwest was the capital of this pastime. The Golden was embraced by many hunters as the dog for the job. Through the mid-1940s half of the Golden litters registered by the American Kennel Club were whelped in southeastern Minnesota.

Forming the GRCA

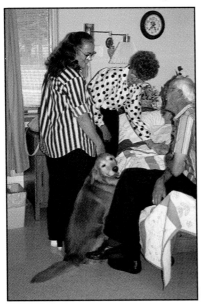

It was through the impetus of the midwestern fanciers that the Golden Retriever Club of America (GRCA) was formed in 1939. Its first president was John K. Wallace. The Club is the guiding force in ensuring that the breed standard, character and original purpose are upheld. The GRCA encourages its members only to breed Goldens that are not only good physical representatives of the breed but are also genetically sound and possess true Golden personalities.

Goldens are happy to shine their love on everyone.

Following World War II the breed saw increased growth, and specimens of the breed could be found in almost every part of the country. A growing number of Americans now had the money and leisure time to include a dog in the family, yet the Golden was still relatively unknown to the general public as a pet. Most were in the hands of show and field competitors or hunters. It was the rare Golden that was found in the average home.

There have been so many dogs and breeders who have been instrumental in shaping the Golden as we know it in the last four decades. Many have been forgotten but several stand out for their contributions to the breed.

In New England, Reinhard Bischoff started Lorelei Kennels. He bred and owned the famous Ch. & Amateur Field Ch. (AFC) Lorelei's Golden Rockbottom UD. As indicated by his titles, Rocky was a dog of immense talent. He was an outstanding sire, a show dog Hall of Famer, a field trial dog and an obedience dog on the side! Lorelei Goldens were bred to be superior specimens of the breed as well as excellent working dogs. Dogs of Reinhard Bischoff's breeding are the foundation for many modern-day Goldens.

Tigathoe Kennels, which is active even today, was started by Mrs. George Flinn, Jr., in the late 1940s. Her Rocky son, Ch. Little Joe of Tigathoe, was one of the breed's most important sires of the 1950s and is behind both field and show lines. Throughout her years in the breed Mrs. Flinn has been active in her fight to keep the Golden a working field dog. Over the years she has owned eight Golden field champions. In the early 1970s she and Mrs. Pat Sadler bred FC-AFC Bonnie Brook's Elmer to Tigathoe's Chickasaw to produce three field champions and the breed's last dual champion (a bench and field champion), Dual Ch. & AFC Tigathoe's Funky Farquar.

American breeders continued to import Goldens from England, and while most had little or no impact on the breed as a whole, in the late 1960s several imports began to make a difference. The greatest change was that coats of lighter color were seen more frequently. Gradually the lighter color became increasingly popular with show fanciers and eventually with the public seeking Goldens. The dogs now imported from England were not only different in color but also in overall type than the darker American Golden that had been developed from English stock of a different era.

During this same period, two half-brothers, Ch. Misty Morn's Sunset CD,TD,WC (Sammy) and Am.-Can.-Bda. (Bermudian) Ch. Cummings' Gold-Rush Charlie forged new records. Sammy has the all-time record for the number of show Goldens produced. Charlie was the all-time high point Golden show dog with 38

FAMOUS OWNERS OF GOLDEN RETRIEVERS

Oprah Winfrey

Mary Tyler Moore

Gerald Ford

Jimmy Stewart

Bill Blass

Ed McMahon

Bob Newhart

Chevy Chase

Frank Gifford

Best-in-Show wins. He was equally important as a sire. His show record was broken in 1993 by Am.-Can. Ch. Asterling's Wild Blue Yonder.

No mention of important dogs during the 1970s would be complete without noting the English import AFC Holway Barty. Barty came to this country when

he was a year old, and his owner, Barbara Howard, soon had him running field trials. He went on to complete his Amateur Field Championship but is best remembered for his contribution in producing working Goldens. He not only produced nine field champions, but many outstanding

Today's Golden is as faithful a friend as his ancestors.

obedience dogs as well. One of his sons, NAFC-FC (National Amateur Field Champion-Field Champion) Topbrass Cotton is the breed's all-time high point field trial Golden and himself the sire of eight field champions as of this writing. Prior to this no Golden had ever produced more than five field champions. Barty added a consistency in marking ability, style and trainability that was lacking in many Golden lines.

Striking Gold in Obedience

It was also in the 1970s that Goldens emerged as one of the premier dogs for obedience competition. When the Obedience Trial Champion title was initiated in July 1977, the first three dogs of any breed to attain it were Golden Retrievers. Since then more Goldens have earned the title than any other breed. Goldens that excel in obedience come from all backgrounds: field, show and pet. The prerequisite is a willing attitude and athletic ability.

As mentioned earlier, Goldens up to this time were not a popular breed. They were a well-kept secret and often confused with Irish Setters. The event that signaled the sudden growth and brought the Golden prominence with the American public was when President Gerald Ford obtained a young Golden female in 1974. Liberty and her subsequent litter of puppies received national publicity. The secret was out. Golden registrations skyrocketed and suddenly the breed was ranked in the top five in popularity, where they continue to hover to this day.

Once primarily sought after for its abilities as a hunting dog, the Golden is now employed in a variety of jobs. They are commonly used by the various organizations that provide sighted guides for the blind, ears for the deaf and service dogs for the handicapped. Many Goldens are well suited to these tasks because of their intelligence, trainability, stability and loyalty. Goldens are also trained and utilized as rescue dogs in numerous situations, such as earthquake relief, avalanches or seeking lost persons. Their natural scenting abilities, along with the power to concentrate on the task at hand make them popular dogs for such work. There is rarely a day that goes by when a Golden isn't seen in a television or magazine ad. They are easy to work with and their expressive faces are good subjects for the media. Goldens have become television stars, with regular roles on several series. *Homeward Bound*, the remake of the 1960s classic *The Incredible Journey*, featured a very wise, gray-faced Golden in one of the three key roles. Goldens have even been the topic of books. *The Leading Lady: Dinah's Story* is the true-life account of actor Tom Sullivan's Seeing Eye dog. It was written by Betty White and Tom

Golden Retrievers excel in obedience competition.

Sullivan. The singer Livingston Taylor has written a children's book about his Golden Retriever entitled *Can I B Good Today?* The book's wonderful illustrations truly capture the personality of Golden Retrievers.

They are owned by famous performers, politicians and even kings. The Golden has become a part of our everyday life and is accessible to everyone.

The All-Purpose Golden

It is important to keep in mind the breed's early history and the original intent and purpose of the Golden as a hunting dog and companion. A common theme of concern has existed among those involved with the welfare and direction of the breed since the 1930s. That worry is that the Golden breed has split into two, three or even more distinct types with different purposes. Unfortunately, this has already occurred to some extent. The Golden has been adapted and bred to succeed in the various phases of dog competition. Not very long ago Goldens that were successful in different activities often came from the same litter. Dogs whose primary purpose was that of a hunting dog could be shown, and many champions were not only good field dogs but produced working dogs as well. While even at that time there were extremes at either end, the breed for the most part was considered dual-purpose. Now, many field dogs no longer resemble Golden Retrievers. The same can be said for many dogs bred strictly for the breed ring, whose excessive bone and coat make them unfit to be working dogs. Serious breeders strive to produce a Golden that fits the standard in all ways and can be used for whatever purposes its owner desires, whether it be as a hunting dog or a family companion. This is the lesson that our breed's history should teach us.

chapter 3

The World
According to the
Golden Retriever

Most of us seek our first Golden Retriever because we are attracted to its physical appearance, reputation as a family dog and overall good temperament. The majority of Goldens live up to these expectations and usually exceed them. As we discuss what can be expected in the behavior of a member of the breed, it must be kept in mind that not all Goldens be-

have similarly. The behavior traits described in this chapter are the reactions of a typical Golden Retriever.

As far as most Goldens are concerned, life is one big party and they are the guests of honor. Almost every human they meet is a part of this bash. There is no doubt about it: Goldens think that people are very special. They will greet anyone, even total strangers, with a wagging tail and a smile—that is, if they are on their best behavior. Sometimes those lacking (or forgetting) their manners are just as likely to leap on their guests to give them a bear hug. It is this love of humans that makes Goldens such enjoyable companions. They want to be in the presence of people, working with them and pleasing them.

Unlike some breeds, which tend to be one-person or single-family oriented, a Golden shares its affections freely with many. He will form an especially strong bond with the person who might be his primary trainer or whoever spends the most time with him, but never to the exclusion of others. This trait, along with a Golden's overt friendliness, is a deterrent to someone seeking a dog that is protective or wary of strangers. Typically, Goldens do not make good guard dogs. They are generally not excessive barkers, though they will alert their owners to unusual incidents such as strange sounds or intruders. While dogs of other breeds might bark, growl and even threaten a stranger, a Golden is most likely to bark and wag its tail in greeting. The old story that the Golden will show the thief where the silver is hidden and then help carry it out is fairly close to the truth.

A Trustworthy Bunch

Goldens naturally seem to trust humans. This is why they are

A DOG'S SENSES

Sight: With their eyes located further apart than ours, dogs can detect movement at a greater distance than we can, but they can't see as well up close. They can also see better in less light, but they can't distinguish many colors.

Sound: Dogs can hear about four times better than we can, and they can hear high-pitched sounds especially well. Their ancestors, the wolves, howled to let other wolves know where they were; our dogs do the same, but they have a wider range of vocalizations, including barks, whimpers, moans and whines.

Smell: A dog's nose is his greatest sensory organ. His sense of smell is so great he can follow a trail that's weeks old, detect odors diluted to one-millionth the concentration we'd need to notice them, even sniff out a person under water!

Taste: Dogs have fewer taste buds than we do, so they're likelier to try anything—and usually do, which is why it's especially important for their owners to monitor their food intake. Dogs are omnivores, which means they eat meat as well as vegetable matter like grasses and weeds.

Touch: Dogs are social animals and love to be petted, groomed and played with.

among the favorite clients of veterinarians, dog groomers and obedience instructors. Along with trust is the inherent ability to forgive. Many owners could learn from their Goldens. A Golden will take a normal correction, given fairly, in stride. He will learn from it and continue to like and respect the person who administered it. A traumatic incident will not affect a Golden for any length of time. He will go on with life, tail wagging.

It is this resiliency and an ability to adapt to new situations that makes the Golden ideal for so many different purposes. Dogs used in guiding the blind, assisting the deaf, providing therapy to old or infirm people—even sharing the media spotlight—must be able to enter any situation or environment and continue to put the tasks of the job ahead of any other distractions. Adaptability makes placing a Golden that may need a new home easier than it is for other breeds. While a Golden may miss its former home and owner, it is seldom apparent to the new owner.

Goldens crave affection and will demand it. As a whole, male members of the breed tend to be more attentive and affectionate than females, who are often more independent in nature. They will want to be petted and then insist that their paws be held for hours at a time. The more insistent ones will stick their noses under an arm and give a forceful nudge until attention is focused totally on them. If you are willing, they will climb in your lap and lie contentedly for hours, forgetting they weigh fifty pounds more than the average lap dog. Licking is an annoying habit some Goldens take to extremes, not just with themselves, but humans as well. They will lick the hands or even a face if it is in reach, and delight in covering it with sloppy kisses.

Goldens just love to retrieve.

When compared with other breeds, Goldens are considered to be among the most trainable. There are stubborn and slow individuals out there, but even these are seldom hopeless. Most Goldens will learn their basic obedience commands with standard training techniques and a minimum of well-timed corrections. They do best if shown what is wanted of them first, rather than being forced into positions. Food treats are a useful motivator to get and hold most Goldens' attention. Yes, Goldens can be easily distracted, as they are often so alert to smells, sights and sounds around them.

Trainability is the Golden's real strength.

Are Goldens intelligent? There are many who swear by the intellectual powers of the Golden. Others refer to them as sweet and dumb. The truth is that when rated against other breeds of dogs, Goldens are in the upper middle when rated on intelligence. When we talk about intelligence in dogs, we are referring to the ability to solve problems and quickness in learning tasks. Intelligence is often confused with trainability, which is the Golden's real strength. There are some extremely intelligent dogs out there, but if they lack trainability and are also stubborn, it can make for a very unpleasant combination. Picture a dog that knows exactly what is wanted and how to do it but refuses because it does not want to please. A dog of average intelligence that wants to please is a much better combination.

The Golden's Nose

Especially powerful is the Golden's nose, which often takes over the function of the brain. One of the main reasons hunters have sought Goldens over the years is for their superior scenting ability. The instinct and desire to use their noses to discover and enjoy new and old smells is ever-present in Goldens. On walks or just in their yard, they are constantly on the alert for smells: It is one of the greatest pleasures of their lives.

The retriever part of the dog's name indicates the type of work for which it was developed. It is also an indication that the average Golden with natural instincts is going to spend a good deal of time looking for and carrying any objects it finds in its mouth. Things suitable for retrieval can be described as anything within reach and not nailed down. Children's toys, books, shoes, socks and dirty underwear are all likely targets for a retriever's mouth. Goldens are known for their gentle mouths, but along the way tooth marks may appear on many of these items. Human arms are a favorite for some Goldens. They will gently reach up and grab the forearm and lead the arm and its owner on a tour of the house. Some Goldens are so happy when they have a particularly wonderful object in their mouths that they make talking sounds.

*Exuberant is
a good word
to describe
a Golden's
character.*

Generally Goldens get along well with other domesticated animals. However, as often as we dislike admitting it, they are dogs and exhibit dog-like traits. While it is not a desirable trait, adult males can be aggressive toward other dogs of the same sex. Occasionally females will exhibit the same tendency. Neutering can help control this problem. Goldens with prey instinct will chase anything that runs from them, such as cats and rabbits—anything small and fast. Chasing larger animals or livestock is usually not a problem; they are more likely to bark at larger animals than chase them, though one can never be certain.

Of particular interest to Goldens is birds. They watch them fly in the air, stalk them in the yard and will jump in the water to swim after ducks. For some, especially those from strong hunting or field backgrounds, it could be called an obsession. If you live in a rural area and keep chickens or ducks, or have an exotic bird in the house, it may be unrealistic for them to coexist without some form of physical separation.

> ## CHARACTERISTICS OF THE GOLDEN RETRIEVER
>
> Loves people—all people
>
> Very trustworthy
>
> Easily adapts to new situations
>
> Highly trainable
>
> Eager retrievers, happy to carry things around
>
> Friendly, outgoing and exuberant

Children and Goldens would seem a natural pair, and most Goldens delight in the companionship of children. However, one should always take precautions in any situation involving a young child and a dog, even one as gentle in character as a Golden. Some Goldens can be intimidated by boisterous youngsters, while others take the abuse and noise in stride. Some Goldens are too active or possessive of objects to be trusted with children. Children can be accidentally injured by being knocked down or playfully grabbed at. Likewise, a child can hurt a young puppy by rough play.

Friendly to a Fault?

Every Golden is a unique individual.

Friendly, outgoing and exuberant in their outlook on life, some Goldens are considered by some to be overly excited or hyper. Due to the very nature of their

design, as medium-size dogs that were bred to work for long periods at a time, they often have a higher level of energy than many breeds. This energy is usually easily controlled, and a normal Golden should calm down quickly. A Golden that is ignored, given little exercise and secluded from attention can develop a behavior that can be described as overexcited. The same dog, if given proper exercise, training and attention, will settle down to a normal level of activity in no time at all.

Certain behaviors should never be tolerated in a Golden. Aggressive actions toward humans, growling, snapping or biting are totally out of character with the breed. The only justification is if circumstances are such that the dog is being hurt or rightfully protecting itself. It is too easy to try to explain the actions of the Golden that bites a hand when removing a food dish or removing something from its mouth as "protecting what is his." In truth, even though they are dogs, this is not acceptable Golden behavior. Goldens should never snap when being groomed or receiving fair corrections in training. What if the next thing the dog bites is a child? Shyness and spookiness are also not in character with the temperament of the Golden. A dog that hides at the sight of visitors or tries to run from anything new is just as much at fault as the aggressive dog. Such an animal can make a satisfactory pet with patience and work, but it should never be bred, as such traits are usually genetic.

Children and Goldens get along very well.

Every Golden is a unique individual with slightly different reactions to life. Some are bold and inquisitive, challenging everything, checking kitchen counters, climbing on kitchen chairs, refusing to take "no" for an answer. Others wait patiently for life to happen, wagging their tails, never even attempting to take something in their mouths without its being given to them. Every one of them has a special trait that distinguishes it from other Golden Retrievers, no matter how many one may have owned. They are truly special creatures in beautiful golden suits. It is safe to say that once a person has owned one, life without a Golden is never the same.

33

MORE INFORMATION ON GOLDEN RETRIEVERS

National Breed Club

Golden Retriever Club of America
Ms. Catherine E. Bird, Secretary
2005 NE 78th Street
Kansas City, MO 64118

The club can give you information on all aspects of the breed, including the names and addresses of breed, obedience and hunting clubs in your area. Inquire about membership.

BOOKS

Bargh, Bernard. *Pet Owner's Guide to the Golden Retriever.* New York: Howell Book House, 1993.

Bauer, Nona Kilgore. *The World of the Golden Retriever.* Neptune, N.J.: TFH Publications, 1993.

Fischer, Gertrude. *The New Complete Golden Retriever.* New York: Howell Book House, 1983.

Foss, Valerie. *Golden Retrievers Today.* New York: Howell Book House, 1994.

Pepper, Jeffrey. *The Golden Retriever.* Neptune, N.J.: TFH Publications, 1985.

Rutherford, Clarice and Loveland, Cherylon. *Retriever Puppy Training, The Right Start for Hunting.* Loveland, Colo.: Alpine Publications, 1988.

Rutherford, Clarice; Branstad, Barbara; and Whicker, Sandy. *Retriever Working Certificate Training.* Loveland, Colo.: Alpine Publications, 1988.

Sucher, Jamie. *Golden Retrievers, A Complete Pet Owner's Manual.* Hauppauge, N.Y.: Barron's Educational Series, 1980.

MAGAZINES

Golden Retriever World, Hoflin Publishing, Inc., 4401 Zephyr Street, Wheat Ridge, Colo. 80033-3299.

VIDEOS

The American Kennel Club. *Golden Retrievers.*

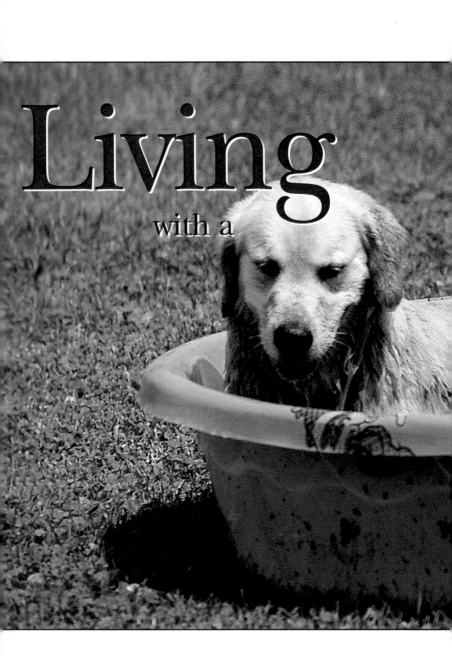

Living

with a

part two

Golden Retriever

chapter 4

Bringing your
Golden Retriever
Home

Before bringing home your new family member, a little planning can help make the transition easier. The first decision to make is where the puppy will live. Will it have access to the entire house or be limited to certain rooms? A similar consideration applies to the yard. It is simpler to control a puppy's activities and to housetrain the puppy if it is confined to definite areas. If doors do not exist where needed, baby gates make satisfactory temporary barriers.

A dog crate is an excellent investment and is an invaluable aid in raising a puppy. Goldens grow to love their crates. They provide a safe, quiet place where a dog can sleep. Used properly, a crate helps with housetraining. The same crate can be used when traveling. A crate that will fit an adult Golden is approximately twenty-four inches wide, thirty-six inches deep and twenty-six inches high. A larger-than-normal dog may be more comfortable in a bigger crate, and a smaller Golden could have a smaller one. Crates are generally made of molded plastic compounds, metal wire or aluminum sheets. They are easily cleaned and last for many years.

Puppy-Proofing

It is definitely easier to raise a puppy than a human baby, but many of the same precautions should be taken. While puppies cannot open cabinets or stick their paws in light sockets, they can get in a lot of trouble with very little effort. Place anything that might be susceptible to puppy teeth or could be broken out of their reach. If possible, all electrical cords should be hidden or secured to floors and walls. Unfortunately such things as tables and chairs cannot be kept out of reach of puppy teeth. If your puppy takes an interest in these, you can buy bitter tasting sprays to apply to those surfaces.

Excessive chewing can be partially resolved by providing a puppy with its own chew toys. There are many such toys and bones available to dog owners, and it can be easy to get carried away with too many toys. Ideal items for Golden pups include stuffed fleece-covered shapes. Goldens love to sink their sharp little teeth into these and carry them around. Braided ropes are fun to pull and shake, and hard rubber balls (never small enough to swallow) are good retrieving objects. It is best to provide a puppy with a few choice toys rather than too many. The more things a puppy has, the more difficult it is to differentiate between what belongs to it and what does not.

Puppies may also get into harmful substances. Anything that is poisonous to humans will harm a dog. Antifreeze tastes sweet and is deadly to animals. Most garden sprays, snail baits and rat poisons are toxic to

**PUPPY
ESSENTIALS**

Your new
puppy will
need:

food bowl

water bowl

collar

leash

I.D. tag

bed

crate

toys

grooming
supplies

dogs, so they must be kept out of reach and used with extreme caution. Another thing to watch out for are the plants in the yard and in the house. Most animals seem to have a sense about staying away from poisonous plants, but it is always wise to be careful. The sharp oxalic crystals in *diffenbachia* (dumb cane) will numb the mouth and cause it to swell if chewed. *Ivies*, if consumed in large amounts, can be toxic. A common ornamental plant in warmer climates, *oleander* is deadly if the branches or leaves are chewed.

There are even things that do not bother humans that are dangerous for dogs. Two of these items are chocolate and salmon from the waters of the Pacific Northwest. A little chocolate is probably harmless, but if consumed in large quantities, it can be fatal. Salmon from the Pacific Northwest contains a fluke that is harmless to humans but will make a dog very ill and even kill it if not treated immediately. Not even cooking makes salmon safe for dogs.

Your puppy will look to you to be her leader.

Chew Toys and Accessories

As a puppy matures and gets its adult teeth, a variety of items made of hard nylon compounds and in a variety of shapes can provide endless hours of chewing enjoyment. As a Golden ages it will continue to enjoy the toys of puppyhood. Anything given to a dog must be large enough that it cannot be swallowed. Rawhide chews should be given with caution. Some dogs are overzealous in trying to swallow the chewed pieces, and, if large enough, these pieces can get lodged in the throat. Rawhides last for a very short period of time and do not have any of the beneficial teeth-cleaning qualities of nylon chews.

Your puppy will need a close-fitting nylon or cotton-webbed collar. This collar should be adjustable so that it can be used for the first couple of months. A properly fitted collar is tight enough that it will not slip over the head, yet an adult finger fits easily under it. A puppy should never wear a choke chain or any other adult training collar. Even when grown, a dog should only wear a choke chain when it is being trained or under direct supervision.

In addition to a collar, you'll need a four-to-six-foot-long leash. One made of nylon or cotton-webbed material is fine as an inexpensive first leash. It need not be more than a half an inch in width. It is important to make sure that the clip is of excellent quality and cannot become unclasped on its own. A retractable leash is another item that is now available to dog owners. The line, which is stored in a hand-held plastic unit, extends up to 15 feet and then shortens immediately with the push of a button. This is ideal when one wants to give a dog more room than a regular leash allows yet still retain control. When a Golden has reached maturity, one may wish to purchase a stronger leash, either of webbed material or leather. Leather is the strongest and will last a long time if properly cared for. As a leather leash is used and ages it becomes supple and is very comfortable in the hand. The width of the leash should be between one-half and one inch and the length between four and six feet.

The final starter items a puppy will need are a water bowl and food dish. You can select a smaller food dish for your puppy and then get a bigger one when your dog matures. Bowls are available in plastic, stainless steel and even ceramic. Stainless steel is probably the best choice, as it is practically indestructible. Plastic bowls deteriorate with age, are chewable and can break. Ceramic bowls, while attractive, are heavy and they chip. A Golden intent on carrying its bowl around will, and if the bowl is ceramic and dropped, it just might break. Non-spill dishes are available for the dog that likes to play in its water. They are also nearly impossible for a dog to pick up and carry. A one-and-a-half-quart bowl is suitable for the amount of food the average Golden might eat at one meal.

HOUSEHOLD DANGERS

Curious puppies and inquisitive dogs get into trouble not because they are bad, but simply because they want to investigate the world around them. It's our job to protect our dogs from harmful substances, like the following:

IN THE HOUSE

cleaners, especially pine oil

perfumes, colognes, aftershaves

medications, vitamins

office and craft supplies

electric cords

chicken or turkey bones

chocolate

some house and garden plants, like ivy, oleander and poinsettia

IN THE GARAGE

antifreeze

garden supplies, like snail and slug bait, pesticides, fertilizers, mouse and rat poisons

The All-Important Routine

Most puppies do best if their lives follow a schedule. They need definite and regular periods of time for playing, eating and sleeping. Puppies like to start their day early. This is a good time to take a short walk or play some retrieving games. After breakfast, most are ready for a nap. How often this pattern is repeated will depend on one's daily routine. Sometimes it is easier for a working person or family to stick with a regular schedule than it is for someone who is home all of the time.

John now gets up at 5:30 A.M., when his new puppy, Max, is ready and waiting impatiently in his own dog room. John greets Max, snaps on his collar and lead, and takes him outside to the potty area of the yard until that business is complete. Then they take a 15-minute walk around the neighborhood. On returning they make another quick visit to the potty area before going inside. While John prepares for work, Max plays with his favorite toy. They eat breakfast together and then, after one last trip outside and a few retrieved balls, Max goes to his room. He naps, plays, drinks water and naps some more. If he has to go potty there is a corner of the room with some newspaper, but he rarely needs to use it. John has changed his lunch schedule and comes home, at which time the morning's routine is repeated. In the late afternoon, when John returns home for the day, they go for another walk or go to the park. They go home for dinner, outside again, and then spend some quiet time together. After one last trip to the potty area, it's bedtime. Max likes the predictability of his life and is a very happy puppy.

Puppies need exercise!

Most Goldens reach their peak of activity and need the least amount of rest from six months to three years of age. As they mature they spend increasingly long periods of time sleeping. It is important to make an effort to ensure that a Golden receives sufficient exercise each day to keep it in proper weight and fitness throughout its life. Puppies need short periods of exercise, but, due to the fact that their bodies are developing, it should never be done to excess. Walks are more suitable for young puppies than running. Anything over one mile should not be attempted unless it is broken by periods of rest. Adult dogs can withstand longer distances, but it is always crucial to keep temperature and the availability of water in mind.

Swimming is an excellent exercise and pastime that many Goldens enjoy. If the weather is seasonable and the water warm, they can be introduced to swimming when they're two or three months old. Some puppies are more willing to enter water if accompanied by a person. Many Goldens will swim after and retrieve sticks out of the water for hours at a time.

Protective Measures

All puppies need some form of identification, even before receiving their rabies shots and being licensed. It's not pleasant to think that your dog could become

lost, but unfortunately it does happen. Most pet stores and veterinary offices have access to sources that make identification tags that can be attached to the puppy's collar. It is more important that the owner's name is on this tag than the dog's name. Collars and tags have been known to come

Dogs and cats can be friends.

off and then, suddenly, all means of identification are gone. An additional protection is to have your dog tattooed when it reaches maturity. The best area for a tattoo is the inside of one of the rear legs, where the hair is sparse. Your driver's license number, social security number or the dog's AKC registration number can be used for identification. The first two are probably the better choices as tracing them is easier. There are tattoo registries that list dogs (see Chapter 13, Resources, for addresses). Another form of identification is a microchip, a rice-grain-sized pellet that is actually implanted under the dog's skin. Identification is made by a sensing device. Tattoos and microchips are excellent forms of I.D.; however, the person who finds a dog may not know to look for a tattoo, and certainly would not know to look for a microchip. Most animal control agencies have the training to look for these forms of identification, but some may not. Consequently, a dog should wear an I.D. tag as well as a tattoo or microchip.

The single best preventative measure one can take to ensure that a dog is not lost or stolen is to provide it with a completely fenced yard. Most Goldens will be contained with a five-to-six-foot-high fence constructed of wire mesh, chain link or wood. Check the fence periodically for digging spots or weakened structure. Besides a fence, added security can be provided by constructing a dog run or kennel. Goldens do not need particularly large runs, as the average adult is content to spend most of its time resting. A five-by-eight-foot area is sufficient. It should be covered to prevent escape and offer protection from the elements. The floor of the run can be cement or gravel. It is not only against city and county ordinances to allow one's dog to roam free, it is also irresponsible dog ownership. While most Goldens are good at staying near their homes, all it takes is one unexpected occurrence for a Golden to be out of its unfenced yard and in potential danger.

Lacey's Story

Throughout her thirteen years, Lacey had always stayed at home, even though her yard only had a three-foot-high fence that the athletic Golden could clear with a single hop. On Christmas Eve a neighbor set off fireworks, and although Lacey was nearly deaf she could pick up the shrill noise of the whistlers. They

Make sure your puppy wears a collar and tags in public.

frightened the old girl, and she ran in terror down the long driveway to the busy road and then wandered, completely disoriented. A woman from a nearby home spotted Lacey. She worked for a veterinarian and had heard the fireworks herself, so she recognized the problem. She caught the old Golden, took her to her

home and checked her collar for a tag. There was a rabies tag, but nothing that said who her owners were or where she lived. As it would be two days before any offices would be open that could help trace the lost dog, Lacey stayed with the woman. She could have spent Christmas with her family if she had had a better form of identification and also an escape-proof yard.

chapter 5

Feeding
your
Golden Retriever

The nutritional needs of a dog will change throughout its lifetime. It is necessary to be aware of these changes not only for proper initial growth to occur, but also so your dog can lead a healthy life for many years.

When a puppy first leaves the home of its breeder it should have been weaned

from its dam for at least one week and should be eating puppy food. Be sure to ask what type of puppy food that is and plan on continuing to use it for at least the first few days your puppy is in its new home. If it's a premium dog food and is readily available where you live, there is no reason not to continue feeding it. If for some reason you wish to switch food, then do so gradually. Ask the breeder to give you several days' supply and gradually mix it in with the new food.

When switching dog foods at any age, follow a definite plan. The first day feed three-fourths old feed to one-fourth of the new. The next day feed a mixture that is half and half. The third day feed three-fourths new and one-fourth old. After that the new feed can be served on its own.

TYPES OF FOODS/TREATS

There are three types of commercially available dog food—dry, canned or semimoist—and a huge assortment of treats (lucky dogs!) to feed your dog. Which should you choose?

Dry and canned foods contain similar ingredients. The primary difference between them is their moisture content. The moisture is not just water. It's blood and broth, too, the very things that dogs adore. So while canned food is more palatable, dry food is more economical, convenient and effective in controlling tartar buildup. Most owners feed a 25% canned/75% dry diet to give their dogs the benefit of both. Just be sure your dog is getting the nutrition he needs (you and your veterinarian can determine this).

Semimoist foods have the flavor dogs love and the convenience owners want. However, they tend to contain excessive amounts of artificial colors and preservatives.

Dog treats come in every size, shape and flavor imaginable, from organic cookies shaped like postmen to beefy chew sticks. Dogs seem to love them all, so enjoy the variety. Just be sure not to overindulge your dog. Factor treats into his or her regular meal sizes.

Life-Stage Feeding

An adolescent dog requires a much higher intake of protein, calories and nutrients than an adult dog due to the demands of its rapidly developing body. Most commercial brands of dry kibble meet these requirements and are well balanced for proper growth. Feeding a homemade diet may not provide the proper balance of needed nutrients. One should only do so with the aid of books on canine nutrition or the guidance of an animal nutritionist. Adding supplements to a well-formulated dog food will destroy the designed balance. For example, the addition of calcium can lead to improper bone growth and result in structural problems. The majority of puppy foods now available are so carefully planned that it is unwise to attempt to add anything other than water to them on a regular basis.

The major ingredients of most dry dog foods are chicken, beef or lamb by-products and corn, wheat or rice. The higher the meat content, the greater the protein percentage, palatability and digestibility of the food. Protein percentages in puppy food are usually between 25 and 40 percent. There are many advantages of dry dog foods over semimoist and canned dog foods for puppies and normal, healthy adult Goldens.

The two best reasons to feed dry food are: (1) Dry food is less expensive than canned food of equal quality. (2) The chewing action involved in eating a dry food is better for the health of the teeth and gums.

Dogs whose diets are based on canned or soft foods have a greater likelihood of developing calcium deposits and gum disease. Canned or semimoist foods do serve certain functions. Due to the higher percentage of meat-based products and higher water content, they are extremely tasty and easy to digest. As a supplement to dry dog food, in small portions, canned or semi-moist foods can be useful to stimulate appetites and increase needed weight gain. But unless very special conditions exist they are not the best way for a dog to meet its food needs.

Your Puppy's Meal Plan

By the time a puppy is about seven weeks old it can easily eat dry dog food. Prior to this age the consistency of the food must be like mush, usually done by soaking in water. This changes dramatically in a matter of days as the teeth grow and jaws strengthen. A Golden puppy should be fed three times a day until it is six months old. How these feedings are spaced out during the day will depend on one's schedule. There is no set rule on the quantity of food to feed. The guidelines printed on the back of dog food bags can help, but they can be misleading. As Goldens can often be ravenous eaters, it is easy for

HOW MANY MEALS A DAY?

Individual dogs vary in how much they should eat to maintain a desired body weight—not too fat, but not too thin. Puppies need several meals a day, while older dogs may need only one. Determine how much food keeps your adult dog looking and feeling her best. Then decide how many meals you want to feed with that amount. Like us, most dogs love to eat, and offering two meals a day is more enjoyable for them. If you're worried about overfeeding, make sure you measure correctly and abstain from adding tidbits to the meals.

Whether you feed one or two meals, only leave your dog's food out for the amount of time it takes her to eat it—10 minutes, for example. Freefeeding (when food is available any time) and leisurely meals encourage picky eating. Don't worry if your dog doesn't finish all her dinner in the allotted time. She'll learn she them to become overweight if the amounts on the food bag are followed closely. There is a fine line between proper growth and excessive weight. The ribs or bones of a puppy should never protrude or be visible. This is a sign that nutritional needs are not being met. Though not visible, when hands are placed on the body of the pup, those ribs should be easy to feel. If the hands sink into the body, then the food amounts should be cut back. A good plan to follow is to divide the amount recommended by three. If the puppy is finishing all three of these portions throughout the day and the appearance of the body indicates proper growth, then stay with those amounts. If the puppy looks like it is gaining excessively then reduce the amount that is given. The same applies for the puppy that leaves quantities of food uneaten, yet is at good weight and energy level otherwise. Obviously if a puppy is eating its rations and appears thin, its food intake should be increased. This is something that can only be accomplished by observation and good judgment. There are Golden pups that could not care less for food. They are more interested in other activities than eating. They will finally eat when it is absolutely necessary, but the result is slower than normal growth and a thin appearance. Sometimes these pups can be taught to appreciate food by the addition of a small amount of canned dog food. Regular meals build an appetite and develop the habit of eating normally.

HOW TO READ THE DOG FOOD LABEL

With so many choices on the market, how can you be sure you're feeding the right food for your dog? The information's all there on the label—if you know what you're looking for.

Look for the nutritional claim right up top. Is the food "100% nutritionally complete?" If so, it's for nearly all life stages; "growth and maintenance," on the other hand, is for early development; puppy foods are marked as such, as are foods for senior dogs.

Ingredients are listed in descending order by weight. The first three or four ingredients will tell you the bulk of what the food contains. Look for the highest-quality ingredients, like meats and grains, to be among them.

The Guaranteed Analysis tells you what levels of protein, fat, fiber and moisture are in the food, in that order. While these numbers are meaningful, they won't tell you much about the quality of the food. Nutritional value is in the dry matter, not the moisture content.

In many ways, seeing is believing. If your dog has bright eyes, a shiny coat, a good appetite and a good energy level, chances are his diet's fine.

While the food does not need to soak in water, the addition of a small amount of water will increase the palatability of the food. Some studies have shown that soaking food for a short period of time prior to being fed increases its digestibility and lessens the chances of gastric disorders such as bloat.

Puppies and dogs should have a place of their own where they can eat their meals without disturbance. If one has obtained a dog crate, this can be an ideal place to feed a dog. If a household consists of more than one dog, it is a wise idea to feed the dogs separately. More dog fights occur over food rights than any other issue. Give a dog a definite period of time to eat its food rather than allowing it to nibble throughout the day. If that food has not been eaten within a ten-minute period, pick it up and do not feed again until the next mealtime. One of the best ways to spot health problems in dogs, and Goldens in particular because they tend to be such good eaters, is monitoring their food intake. Most Goldens that miss a meal under normal circumstances are not well.

Golden Retrievers rarely skip their meals.

Unlike humans, dogs do not need variety in their diet. Every one of their meals is balanced. They should be kept on the same feed unless a change of diet is warranted. Some owners like to spice up their dogs' life with human food. Table scraps and leftovers given occasionally will not interfere with most dogs' appreciation of their regular food, but if a dog cons its owner into believing it needs such additions to eat, then the practice should be stopped immediately. Most dogs only have to miss a couple of meals before they realize they can eat without the addition of special ingredients. Scraps given regularly can lead to weight gain if the amount of the dog's regular food is not reduced. The risk of destroying the nutritional balance of the dog food also exists. Some human foods fed in large quantities can lead to gastrointestinal problems, which can result in loose stools and even diarrhea.

From six months to a year of age the puppy should remain on puppy food but the feedings should decrease to twice a day. By the time a dog reaches a year of age it should be switched to an adult maintenance diet. The number of feedings can remain at twice a day, though it is easier for most owners to feed a large meal once a day. A dog that is prone to digestive problems may be better off with two smaller meals. Anytime the food a dog is eating is changed, follow the schedule discussed in the beginning of the chapter to allow your dog's digestive system to adjust to the new feed.

Your Golden should have cool, fresh water at all times.

If a dog is very active, a canine athlete, so to speak, one may want to use a food with a higher protein content than normal, 28% for example. As dogs mature and slow down they no longer have the protein or caloric needs of younger dogs. The ingredients of the food should reflect these changes. The ratio of grain to meat products should increase. Whether one selects a feed based on corn, wheat, rice or one of the three meat sources is often a personal preference. Some dogs are allergic to certain grains and meats and this will directly affect what they can eat. Such allergies are indicated by skin problems or an inability to properly digest the food. This can be confirmed by veterinary tests. Lamb- and rice-based foods are considered to be the least allergenic and most easily digestible for dogs with allergies to other food sources.

The amount of food an adult Golden should eat daily will vary according to the size of the dog, its activity level and how much time it spends outside. If all other factors are equal, a dog that spends a large amount of time outside will require more food in colder months than when it is warm. A small female Golden in the fifty-pound range of moderate activity living in a mild climate may only need three cups of quality maintenance dog food per day. A large male under the same circumstances may consume five to six cups and stay in good weight. There is no need to add cooked eggs, cottage cheese or oils to the diet. Most dog foods contain everything a dog will need. As always, one's eyes and hands are the best guide to the physical condition of the dog and what he may need.

TO SUPPLEMENT OR NOT TO SUPPLEMENT?

If you're feeding your dog a diet that's correct for her developmental stage and she's alert, healthy-looking and neither over- nor underweight, you don't need to add supplements. These include table scraps as well as vitamins and minerals. In fact, a growing puppy is in danger of developing musculoskeletal disorders by oversupplementation. If you have any concerns about the nutritional quality of the food you're feeding, discuss them with your veterinarian.

Most Golden owners should consider placing their dog on a food that is very low in fat and protein content by the age of eight or nine, unless the dog is still very active. A dog that is inactive either by choice or the owner's laziness has lower nutritional requirements. Another thing to keep in mind is that as dogs age, their kidneys can be destroyed if kept on a food with a high protein content. The problem is that when the amount fed is reduced to the dog's actual needs, the dog thinks it is being starved to death. Consequently foods formulated for older dogs are low in fat and protein content (as low as 8 percent and below 18 percent in protein). The amount of actual bulk is increased so that the dog still believes it is eating something.

Maintaining the proper weight and nutrition of an older Golden is probably more difficult than at any other stage of life. A certain amount of body fat is necessary to protect him in the event of illness. Too much excess weight will make the dog even less active and more prone to physical problems. Leftovers given to an older dog will often upset his digestive system for days. The same food would not even bother a younger dog. If a dog develops such problems as kidney failure, heart disease or an overly sensitive digestive tract, there are specially formulated foods commercially available. These will continue to meet the nutritional needs of a dog without further aggravating the physiological problem.

The physical appearance a Golden presents is as much a result of genetics as it is the food it eats. The owner that feeds a dog quality food and keeps him in optimum weight for his size will be rewarded with a Golden whose health and fitness mirrors his diet.

Grooming
your
Golden Retriever

As a breed, Goldens require a minimum amount of regular grooming to remain clean and attractive. A little brushing, an occasional bath and a bit of trimming pretty much cover the needs of a Golden. However, while your Golden should never need the services of a professional groomer, life isn't always so simple.

Grooming should begin while a dog is a puppy and should become routine. Some breeders clip puppy nails weekly until they go to their new homes. This makes nursing more comfortable for the dam and teaches the puppy to accept having its nails clipped. Some breeders also use a fine-toothed comb daily to remove dirt from the coats. Mouths and baby teeth are checked to see how bites are developing, and ears are observed for cleanliness. All of these preliminary steps taken by the breeder will help make grooming easier for the new owner as long as the process is continued.

Getting Started

A well-groomed Golden is a handsome dog.

For starters, one will need a small slicker brush and a fine-toothed comb. Slicker brushes consist of a series of row after row of tiny metal wires that sit on a flat or slightly curved surface that is attached to a handle. The wires are usually all slightly bent in the same direction. A fine-toothed comb, often called a flea comb, removes dirt and fleas. When a puppy is young it is a good idea to brush and/or comb it daily. If a puppy is not already used to having its nails clipped it is best to do this now rather than waiting and battling a seventy-pound dog. Human nail clippers can be used on puppies until they are about three months old. These make it easier to remove just the tips of tiny nails. Be sure to clip the dewclaws if these have not been removed.

Check your Golden's ears regularly, and even if they do not look dirty, get him used to having a cotton swab soaked in a little ear cleaner run around the inside of the ear. Lift up your dog's lips and inspect the mouth. Your puppy will become used to being examined and having sensitive parts of its body handled, and you will learn what is normal for your dog, making it easier to spot potential problems before they require more serious attention.

How much coat care the adult Golden requires will depend on the type of coat it carries. A heavily coated dog with lots of feathering will need more upkeep than a dog with less coat and sparse feathers. A Golden should have at least one session of brushing per week unless circumstances require more frequent care. All kinds of brushes, shedders and matt splitters are available, but all that is really needed is a large slicker brush and a comb. Areas that require special attention are the feathers of the front and rear legs, the tail feathers and the fine hair just underneath and behind the ears. All of these areas are prone to matting due to scratching, chewing or things getting caught in the longer hair.

Golden's love water—especially when it's hot out!

Goldens shed their coats twice a year. When this occurs will depend on the climate in your area. When your dog sheds, its fine undercoat is lost *en masse*, often in clumps. During periods of shedding, you may wish to brush your dog several times a day to keep the fine undercoat from ending up all over the house and yard.

You can help loosen up that dead coat by running your hands and fingers through it, massaging the skin. Some say this helps stimulate new coat growth. Regardless, it helps to speed the shedding process and is enjoyable for the dog. Combs are useful for the feathers and area under the ears where matts collect. It is difficult if not impossible to get a flea comb through an adult coat unless the dog has recently shed.

Taking a Bath

Goldens should be bathed no more than every six to eight weeks, and even this may be unnecessary on a

**GROOMING
TOOLS**

pin brush

slicker brush

flea comb

towel

matt rake

grooming
glove

scissors

nail clippers

tooth-
cleaning
equipment

shampoo

conditioner

clippers

shorter-coated dog that swims frequently. Certain skin conditions may warrant more frequent bathing with specially treated or medicated shampoos. Excessive bathing can destroy the natural balance of oils of your Golden's skin and coat. Human shampoos should never be used on dogs. They are formulated for the pH of human hair and skin, which is quite different from that of a dog. There are many shampoos available that are specifically designed for dogs. If in doubt as to what to use, call a grooming shop and find out what they recommend. Be careful selecting varieties sold in markets and convenience stores, as they are often too harsh for a dog's coat.

Prior to bathing a dog be sure it is well brushed and free of matts. Matts left in the coat will become even tighter and harder to remove if they go through the bathing process. Baths work best if lukewarm water is used; however, cold water is fine if the weather is warm. Wet the dog thoroughly and then apply the shampoo, making sure to keep it out of the eyes and ears. You can put cotton balls in the ears to keep excess water out. When rinsing, be sure to get all the soap out. Keep rinsing even after all of the soap appears to be gone. Soap left on the dog can irritate its skin. More damage is done to the skin and coat by too frequent bathings and soap left on to dry than by leaving a dog dirty.

If the dog is being washed with a flea shampoo, remember that the suds will need to sit on the dog for several minutes before they are rinsed off. A flea shampoo only kills the fleas that are on the dog at the time it is being bathed. Once it is rinsed off, the fleas will be back on the dog. If a flea dip is applied it should be done after the soap has been rinsed out. Flea dips are only effective if a dog is clean.

After its bath, towel your dog off to remove excess water. Most Goldens will shake wildly at some time during and after the bath and get you completely wet. If it is a warm day a dog can be left to dry on its own; in colder weather use a hand-held hair dryer set at low heat.

Don't Neglect Nails

Trimming nails is essential for the well-being of your dog's feet. Dogs that receive lots of exercise or that are on cement may wear their nails down enough on their own that clipping is practically unnecessary. But even these dogs as they become older and less active will need nail care. Normally, nails should be trimmed every two weeks or when the nails start to touch the floor. This is noticeable as a clicking sound when the dog walks on hard surfaces. Long nails will scratch floors and get caught in carpeting. Dogs can have difficulty walking on long nails. From a health standpoint, nails that are allowed to become long for any period of time will break down the structure of the foot by causing the toes to spread out and splay the foot. Long nails are also more likely to split and require veterinary care.

This Golden has been groomed to perfection.

Nail clippers come in two basic styles. One type has two blades and works like a pair of scissors. The other style has an oblong opening that the nail fits in and a single blade that cuts the nail when the movable handle is squeezed. Either variety works well. Besides large-sized nail clippers, you should buy a commercially available styptic powder specifically for dog nails. Keep it on hand in case you cut a nail too short. The blood vessel in a nail is referred to as the quick and serves as the blood supply to the nail. If the tip of the quick is cut, it will bleed. Golden owners are fortunate, as the nails of Goldens

are light colored, somewhat opaque and the vein is visible when the nail is viewed from the side. To be safe, only cut the hook part of the nail until you're more confident. Most of the time a minor cut to the quick will stop bleeding on its own. The styptic powder will stop the bleeding; and if it doesn't, applying the powder along with some pressure does the job. If clipping nails is a scary proposition for you, most groomers and veterinary clinics will take care of it for a small fee.

Caring for Ears, Teeth and Coat

Your Golden's ears will need weekly cleaning. Even if they do not appear dirty, frequent care will prevent ear problems. Ear-cleaning solutions are available in pet stores. Place several drops in each ear and massage the ears for a half a minute. This way the solution can penetrate the greasy dirt. Let the dog shake its head to loosen the dirt. To actually remove the dirt, use cotton swabs or cotton balls. Clean the exterior areas of the inside of the ear, getting into the nooks and crannies of the outer ear. A need for more frequent cleanings may require veterinary attention.

Your Golden's teeth need regular brushing.

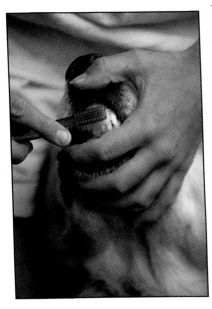

We rarely think about the cleanliness of our dog's teeth, leaving that to the natural cleansing action of chewing. Dogs, especially as they grow older, develop gum disease and tooth degeneration just like humans. We can help counter this progression by providing regular care by brushing the teeth. Canine toothpastes and toothbrushes are available and can be used daily.

The final grooming consideration for a Golden is trimming its hair. For this, the only thing you need is a pair of hair scissors. The most obvious area of trimming for a Golden is its feet, where some dogs grow an unnecessary amount of hair. The hair should be trimmed so that it is even around the edge of the pads along the outer edge and bottom of the foot. Hair that sticks out between the toes may also be trimmed. It is not only neater in appearance, but the feet will track less dirt into the house and are easier to wipe clean. If leg feathers are excessively long, you may want to trim them so they are less likely to bring in twigs, leaves and other useless items. Some people trim the feathers severely to make upkeep easier. Matts can be combed out if they are small, or they can be carefully scissored out.

Many Goldens that have been spayed or neutered grow a longer-than-normal undercoat that extends beyond the outer guard coat. It is light and fluffy in appearance and is most prominent on the rear legs and shoulders. It often makes little matts or tangles and can require extra brushing. It is simple to trim this hair so that it is flush with the rest of the coat. It is not only more attractive but will need less work.

Goldens are very easy to keep well groomed, and only serious neglect should get a Golden to the point where it needs a professional groomer. Goldens enjoy being groomed. They love the attention and seem to know that you are helping them stay beautiful and healthy.

chapter 7

Keeping your
Golden Retriever
Healthy

The strongest body and soundest genetic background will not help a dog lead a healthy life unless it receives regular attention from its owner.

Dogs are susceptible to infections, parasites and diseases for which they have no natural immunity. It is up to us to take preventative measures to make sure that none of these interferes with our dog's health. It may help to think of the upkeep of a dog's health in relation to the calendar. Certain things need to be done on a weekly, monthly and annual basis.

Weekly grooming can be the single best monitor of a dog's overall health. The actual condition of the coat and skin and the "feel" of the body can indicate good health or potential problems. Grooming will help you discover small lumps on or under the skin in the early stages before they become large enough to be seen without close examination.

You will spot fleas and ticks when brushing the coat and examining the skin. In some parts of the country and at certain times of the year they can be a dog owner's number one enemy. Besides harboring diseases and parasites, they can make daily life a nightmare for some dogs.

Many Goldens are severely allergic to even a couple of fleas on their bodies. They scratch, chew and destroy their coat and skin because of fleas. Other Goldens can be covered with fleas and one would never be aware of it without actually examining the dog. Even if the fleas are not actually seen, their existence can be confirmed by small black specks in the coat. These are the flea feces; when a dog is bathed, they dissolve, making the water a rusty red.

Flea Control

Flea control is never a simple endeavor. The flea lives outside and hops on the dog not only for travel purposes but also for nutrition. Dogs bring fleas inside, where they lay eggs in the carpeting and furniture—anywhere your dog goes in the house. Consequently, real control is a matter of not only treating the dog but also the other environments the flea inhabits. The yard can be sprayed, and in the house, sprays and flea bombs can be used, but there are more choices for the dog. Flea sprays are effective for one to two weeks depending on their ingredients. Dips applied to the dog's coat following a bath have equal periods of effectiveness. The disadvantage to both of these is that some dogs may have problems with the chemicals.

These specks in your dog's fur mean he has fleas.

Flea collars can be effective, as they prevent the fleas from traveling to your dog's head, where it's moister and more hospitable. Dog owners tend to leave flea collars on their dogs long after they've ceased to be effective. Again, some dogs may have problems with flea collars, and children should never be allowed to handle them.

FIGHTING FLEAS

Remember, the fleas you see on your dog are only part of the problem—the smallest part! To rid your dog and home of fleas, you need to treat your dog *and* your home. Here's how:

- Identify where your pet(s) sleeps. These are "hot spots."

- Clean your pets' bedding regularly by vacuuming and washing.

- Spray "hot spots" with a non-toxic, long-lasting flea larvicide.

- Treat outdoor "hot spots" with insecticide.

- Kill eggs on pets with a product containing insect growth regulators (IGRs).

- Kill fleas on pets per your veterinarian's recommendation.

Some owners opt for a product that can work from the inside out. Veterinarians can apply a chemical to a spot on your dog's coat. The chemical is absorbed into the dog's body and works for up to a month to repel fleas. Another such option is a pill (prescribed by a veterinarian) that you give to the dog on a regular basis in its food. The chemicals in the pill course through the dog's bloodstream, and when a flea bites, the blood kills the flea.

Some worry that placing so many poisonous chemicals in our dogs' bodies does more long-term damage than any flea. While there are no studies to support this fear, one cannot help but be concerned. Use of one type of chemical flea control often precludes the use of another. The directions and precautions should always be checked prior to use.

Natural forms of flea control include the addition of brewer's yeast and garlic to the diet. There are flea collars made of seeds from eucalyptus trees, and organic-based flea shampoos, dips and sprays that have short-term effectiveness.

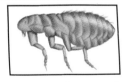

The flea is a die-hard pest.

Going over a dog thoroughly every day with a flea comb works wonders. Getting a fine-toothed comb through an adult Golden's coat can be nearly impossible, though. It really comes down to a decision based on how much of a problem fleas actually are for the dog in question and what an owner feels most comfortable using.

Proper Ear Care

Another weekly job is cleaning the ears (for "how to" advice, see Chapter 6). Goldens do not have the ear problems common to dogs with long pendulous or hairy ears. Even so, the moist environment created by ears that hang over the opening is a favorite place for infections to incubate.

Three types of ticks (l-r): the wood tick, brown dog tick and deer tick.

Many times an ear problem is evident if a dog scratches its ears or shakes its head frequently. Clean ears are less likely to develop problems, and if they do occur, they will be spotted while they can be treated easily. If a dog's ears are very dirty and seem to need cleaning on a daily basis, it is a good indication that something else is going on in the ears besides ordinary dirt and the normal accumulation of earwax. A visit to the veterinarian may indicate a situation that needs special medication.

Brushing Teeth

Regular brushing of the teeth often does not seem necessary when a dog is young and spends much of its time chewing; the teeth always seem to be immaculately clean. As a dog ages, it becomes more important to brush the teeth daily.

Calcium deposits accumulate primarily on the back upper molars but spread to all but the incisors in older dogs. These deposits are known as calculus or tartar and are the leading cause of gum disease, which leads to the eventual loss of teeth. Daily brushings can slow down this process, but even regular brushing does not totally halt the formation of calculus.

To help prolong the health of your dog's mouth, he should have his teeth cleaned twice a year at a veterinary clinic. Observing the mouth regularly, checking for the formation of abnormalities or broken teeth, can lead to early detection of oral cancer or infection.

One of the worst enemies of a Golden's teeth is the habit of chewing on its coat. The coarse hairs wear down the front teeth like nothing else it might chew. In many middle-aged to older dogs the incisors may even wear down to the gum. The only way to prevent this from occurring is to stop the dog from chewing.

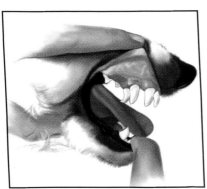

Check your dog's teeth frequently and brush them regularly.

Keeping Nails Short

The nails on all feet should be kept short enough so they do not touch the ground when the dog walks. There are several concerns involved with the nails. The first is the condition of our hard floors and carpeting. More importantly, though, is the comfort of the dog.

Dogs with long nails can have difficulty walking on hard or slick surfaces. This can be especially true of older dogs. As nails grow longer, the only way the foot can compensate and retain balance is for the toes themselves to spread apart, causing the foot itself to become flattened and splayed. Over periods of time this will have a permanent effect and destroy the structure of the foot. Not only is the foot now broken down, but the legs themselves and the entire body of the dog are affected. In effect, the dog can be crippled.

Nails that are allowed to become long are also more prone to splitting. This is painful to the dog and usually requires surgical removal of the remainder of the nail for proper healing to occur. (See Chapter 6 for more on nail care.)

Keeping Eyes Clear

A Golden's eyes rarely need special attention. A small amount of matter in the corner of the eye is normal, as is a bit of "tearing." Goldens with eyelashes that turn inward (trichiasis) and rub against the eye itself often exhibit more tearing than normal due to the irritation to the eyes. These eyelashes can be surgically removed if it appears to be a problem, but are often ignored.

Excessive tearing can be an indication that a tear duct is blocked. This, too, can be corrected by a simple surgical procedure. Eye discharge that is thicker and mucous-like in consistency is often a sign of some type of eye infection or actual injury to the eye. This can be verified by a veterinarian, who will provide a topical ointment to place in the corner of the eye. Most minor eye injuries heal quickly if proper action is taken.

Checking Anal Sacs

A dog's anal sacs, located under the skin on both sides of the anal opening, should be checked periodically. These fill with a fluid that is very smelly and normally light brown and thin in consistency. Removing the fluid in these sacs is termed *expressing*. A good time to express the anal sacs is during a dog's bath. It can be done at other times but can be messier.

A sign that a dog is having problems with its anal sacs is when it scoots on its bottom across the floor. When the sacs are impacted they become swollen, and the fluid is very dark and viscous. Serious impaction can lead to infection and require surgery. Needless to say, it is quite uncomfortable for the dog.

The sacs are expressed by placing the thumb and the index and third fingers of one hand on both sides of the outer edge of the anus. Strong inward squeezing pressure on both sides of the anus at the same time usually removes the smelly contents of the sac. A paper towel should be kept in the hand that is squeezing to collect the fluid.

If a male dog has not been neutered his testicles should be checked regularly for the formation of tumors. This becomes increasingly common as a dog becomes older. An unspayed female is prone to mammary tumors, so the areas around the nipples should be felt for lumps. These tumors are often malignant and shorten an otherwise healthy dog's life.

YOUR PUPPY'S VACCINES

Vaccines are given to prevent your dog from getting an infectious disease like canine distemper or rabies. Vaccines are the ultimate preventive medicine: they're given before your dog ever gets the disease so as to protect him from the disease. That's why it is necessary for your dog to be vaccinated routinely. Puppy vaccines start at eight weeks of age for the five-in-one DHLPP vaccine and are given every three to four weeks until the puppy is sixteen months old. Your veterinarian will put your puppy on a proper schedule and will remind you when to bring in your dog for shots.

Vaccines

All dogs need yearly vaccinations to protect them from common deadly diseases. The DHL vaccine, which protects a dog from distemper, hepatitis and leptospirosis, is given for the first time at about seven weeks of age. Another booster is given a few weeks later. After this, a dog should be vaccinated every year throughout its life.

Since the mid-1970s, parvovirus and coronavirus have been the cause of death for thousands of dogs. Puppies and older dogs are most frequently affected by these illnesses. Fortunately, vaccines for these are routinely given now on a yearly basis in combination with the DHL shot.

Kennel cough, though rarely dangerous in a healthy dog that receives proper treatment, can be annoying. It can be picked up anywhere that large numbers of dogs congregate, such as veterinary clinics, grooming shops, boarding kennels, obedience classes or dog shows. The Bordatella vaccine, given twice a year, will protect a dog from getting most strains of kennel cough. It is often not routinely given, so it may be necessary to request it.

In many parts of the country **Lyme disease** is becoming an increasing problem for both dogs and humans. It is carried by the tiny deer tick, whose bite can infect the host. Most tick bites result in an area of red swelling, but the Lyme-infected bite is particularly large, long lasting and painful. Later symptoms include lameness, fatigue and eventual death. There is a protective available for dogs. Check with your veterinarian to be sure he or she thinks it's worthwhile for your dog.

Internal Parasites

While the exterior part of a dog's body hosts fleas and ticks, the inside of the body is commonly inhabited by a variety of parasites. Most of these

are in the worm family. Tapeworms, roundworms, whipworms, hookworms and heartworm all plague our canine friends. There are also several types of protozoa, mainly *coccidia* and *giardia,* that cause problems.

Common internal parasites (l-r): roundworm, whipworm, tapeworm and hookworm.

The common **tapeworm** is acquired by the dog eating infected fleas or lice. In the adult stage the worm inhabits the intestine, where it sucks the nutrients it needs from the dog. Normally one is not aware that a healthy dog even has tapeworms. The only clues may be a dull coat, a loss of weight despite a good appetite or occasional gastrointestinal problems.

Confirmation is by the presence of worm segments in the stool. These appear as small, pinkish-white, flattened rectangular-shaped pieces. When dry, they look like rice. If segments are not present, diagnosis can be made by the discovery of eggs when a stool sample is examined under a microscope. Ridding a dog temporarily of tapeworm is easy with a worming medicine prescribed by a veterinarian. Over-the-counter wormers are not effective for tapeworms and may be dangerous. Long-term tapeworm control is not possible unless the flea situation is also handled.

Ascarids are the most common **roundworm** (nematode) found in dogs. Adult dogs that have roundworms rarely exhibit any symptoms that would indicate the worm is in their body. These worms are cylindrical in shape and may be as long as four to five inches. They do pose a real danger to puppies, where they are usually passed from the mother through the uterus to the unborn puppies.

It is wise to assume that all puppies have roundworms. In heavy infestations they will actually appear in the puppy stools, though their presence is best diagnosed by a stool sample. Treatment is easy and can begin as early as two weeks of age and administered every two weeks thereafter until eggs no longer appear in a stool sample or dead worms are not found in the stool following treatment. Severely infected puppies can die from roundworm infestation. Again, the worming medication should be obtained through a veterinarian.

Hookworm is usually found in warmer climates and infestation is generally from ingestion of larvae from the ground or penetration of the skin by larvae. Hookworms feed in the dog's intestine and can cause anemia, diarrhea and emaciation. As these worms are very tiny and not visible to the eye, their diagnosis must be made by a veterinarian.

Whipworms live in the large intestine and cause few if any symptoms. Dogs usually become infected when they ingest larvae in contaminated soil. Again diagnosis and treatment should all be done by a veterinarian. One of the easiest ways to control these parasites is by picking up stools on a daily basis. This will help prevent the soil from becoming infested.

The protozoa can be trickier to diagnose and treat. **Coccidiosis and giardia** are the most common, and primarily affect young puppies. They are generally associated with overcrowded, unsanitary conditions and can be acquired from the mother (if she is a carrier), the premises themselves (soil) or even water.

The most common symptom of protozoan infection is mucous-like blood-tinged feces. It is only with freshly collected samples that diagnosis of this condition can be made. With coccidiosis, besides diarrhea, the puppies will appear listless and lose their appetite. Puppies often harbor the protozoa and show no symptoms unless placed under stress. Consequently, many times a puppy will not become ill until it goes to its new home. Once diagnosed, treatment is quick and effective and the puppy returns to normal almost immediately.

Heartworm

The most serious of the common internal parasites is the heartworm. At one time it was only found in a small portion of the country but has since spread to almost every region. A dog that is bitten by a mosquito infected with the heartworm *microfilaria* (larvae) will develop worms that are six to twelve inches long. As these worms mature they take up residence in the dog's heart.

The symptoms of heartworm may include coughing, tiring easily, difficulty breathing and weight loss. Heart failure and liver disease may eventually result. Verification of heartworm infection is done by drawing blood and screening for the microfilaria. If a dog tests positive, it is a good idea, especially if no symptoms exist, to have the dog tested again because treatment for heartworm is not only very expensive, it is also dangerous to the life of the dog if not done correctly.

A healthy dog is full of life.

In areas where heartworm is a risk, it is best to place a dog on a preventative, usually a pill given once a month. Because the microfilaria and mosquitoes require warm temperatures to propagate, concern for heartworm transmission is limited to the warmer months of the year. Consequently, many owners only give their dogs the heartworm preventative for a portion of the year. Anytime a dog is taken off heartworm preventative and then placed back on it, it must have its blood checked to make sure it is not harboring heartworm.

At least once a year a dog should have a full veterinary examination. The overall condition of the dog can be observed and a blood sample collected for a complete yearly screening. This way the dog's thyroid functions can be tested, and the job the dog's organs are doing can be monitored. If there are any problems, this form of testing can spot trouble areas while they are easily treatable.

Proper care, regular vaccinations, periodic stool checks and preventative medications for such things as heartworm will all help ensure your dog's health.

Spaying/Neutering

Spaying a female dog or neutering a male is another way to make sure they lead long and healthy lives. Females spayed at a young age have almost no risk of developing mammary tumors or reproductive prob-

lems. Neutering a male is an excellent solution to dog aggression and also removes the chances of testicular cancer.

Female Goldens usually experience their first heat cycle somewhere between six months and one year of age. Unless spayed

Goldens are hairy and often very active.

they will continue to come into heat on a regular cycle. The length of time between heats varies, with anything from every six months to a year being normal.

There is absolutely no benefit to a female having a first season before being spayed, nor in letting her have a litter. Motherhood will have no permanent or beneficial effect on a dog's personality. The decision to breed any female dog and especially a Golden should never be taken lightly. The obvious considerations are whether she is a good physical specimen of the breed and has a sound temperament. There are several genetic problems that are common to Goldens, such as hip dysplasia, cataracts, subaortic stenosis (SAS), von Willebrands disease (VWD) and thyroid. Responsible breeders screen for these prior to making breeding decisions. If a Golden is afflicted with any one of these, he or she should never be considered as a breeding prospect.

Finding suitable homes for puppies is another serious consideration. Due to their popularity, many people are attracted to Goldens and seek puppies without realizing the drawbacks of the breed. They are not always the perfect, well-behaved dogs seen on television. They are hairy, often very active and need lots of personal attention.

Owning a dog is a lifetime commitment to that animal. There are so many unwanted dogs—and yes, even unwanted Goldens—that people must be absolutely sure that they are not just adding to the pet overpopulation problem. Breeding a litter of puppies is not a sure way to make money. In fact, it is more likely that you will lose more than you will ever make when time, effort, equipment and veterinary costs are factored in.

Spaying a female dog relieves the owner from the worries involved with keeping her isolated during her heats, from unwanted litters, and from the headaches associated with breeding puppies.

Many of the same considerations apply to choosing not to neuter a male Golden. They, too, must meet the

---

ADVANTAGES OF SPAY/NEUTER

The greatest advantage of spaying (for females) or neutering (for males) your dog is that you are guaranteed your dog will not produce puppies. There are too many puppies already available for too few homes. There are other advantages as well.

ADVANTAGES OF SPAYING

No messy heats.

No "suitors" howling at your windows or waiting in your yard.

Decreased incidences of pyometra (disease of the uterus) and breast cancer.

ADVANTAGES OF NEUTERING

Lessens male aggressive and territorial behaviors, but doesn't affect the dog's personality. Behaviors are often owner-induced, so neutering is not the only answer, but it is a good start.

Prevents the need to roam in search of bitches in season.

Decreased incidences of urogenital diseases.

same criteria of health and soundness if used to sire a litter. The owner of a male dog has no control over where the resulting puppies will be placed. Yet when it comes to problems that may arise as those puppies grow to adulthood, the owner of the sire is in truth just as responsible as the owner of the dam for the well-being of the offspring.

If a male Golden shows signs of aggression toward other dogs, neutering will almost always correct this situation. Many males let the presence of a female in season, whether it is in their house or just the neighborhood, completely disrupt their lives. They howl, they seek ways to escape their yards and they stop eating all together. A neutered male will not be affected by this type of occurrence, and all in all will be a nicer dog to live with.

Should You Call the Vet?

Throughout a dog's life there are times when an owner must decide whether certain conditions require veterinary attention. Many times there is no doubt, as in the case of serious injury, but other decisions are less clear-cut. Owners should always have a good idea of what is normal for their dogs so that they have a basis for comparison when an abnormal situation is suspected. "Normal" includes appearance, energy, eating and elimination patterns, pulse and temperature. Establish your dog's normal temperature at different times of the day to use as a guideline. **Take your dog's temperature with a rectal thermometer.** Be sure to shake it down to 96 degrees and place a small amount of petroleum jelly

---

WHEN TO CALL THE VET

In any emergency situation, you should call your veterinarian immediately. You can make the difference in your dog's life by staying as calm as possible when you call and by giving the doctor or the assistant as much information as possible before you leave for the clinic. That way, the vet will be able to take immediate, specific action to remedy your dog's situation.

Emergencies include acute abdominal pain, suspected poisoning, snakebite, burns, frostbite, shock, dehydration, abnormal vomiting or bleeding, and deep wounds. You are the best judge of your dog's health, as you live with and observe him every day. Don't hesitate to call your veterinarian if you suspect trouble.

on the tip prior to insertion. It is easiest to do this if the dog is standing.

Lift up the tail and carefully insert the bulb end of the thermometer about one and a half inches into the anal opening. Don't let go, but leave it in for two to three minutes for the most accurate reading. The normal range for a healthy adult dog is 100 to 102.5 degrees.

A dog's **pulse,** which is the same as its heartbeat, is taken by feeling the femoral artery, which is located in the groin region where the leg and body meet. The normal pulse is 70 to 130 beats per minute. It will vary according to the size of the dog and is faster in puppies than adults. A very athletic dog may have a slower pulse than normal. Knowing these two indicators of the dog's internal system is an invaluable aid in determining illness or infection.

Some problems are harder to pinpoint. If a dog's gait is off or there is a noticeable limp, there are many possibilities to consider. If the cause of injury is actually seen when it occurs, we then know its origins. How treatment is approached depends on the severity of the injury. If a dog is completely unable to use a leg we might suspect a break, which would require immediate attention. If the injury does not seem that serious but the dog has problems walking and the limb or area in question is painful, swollen and feels warm to the touch, we can suspect an infection. Both need veterinary attention. Pulled muscles and sprains heal on their own, but a dog must be kept inactive so the area isn't stressed.

Lameness

A limp that appears from nowhere and gets progressively worse is cause for concern. The first thing to do is try to ascertain where the problem actually is. Check the legs and feet for any areas of tenderness, swelling or infection. There are numerous possibilities to consider. In young, developing dogs, lameness in the rear can be an indication of hip dysplasia.

Hip dysplasia is a malformation of the ball and socket joint of the hips and can affect one or both sides of the dog. As a dog ages these joints wear down, and eventually arthritis is associated with the disease. Hip dysplasia can only be properly diagnosed by X-ray. Mild and even many moderate cases of hip dysplasia are usually never suspected until a dog is x-rayed for breeding purposes at two years of age. These X-rays are sent to the Orthopedic Foundation for Animals for evaluation, and only those dogs that receive a fair, good or excellent rating should be bred.

If X-rays do confirm hip dysplasia, there are several considerations. Surgery is one alternative in more serious cases; the pectinius muscle can be split or the femoral head removed. In very serious cases the hips themselves are removed and replaced with Teflon hips. Most mildly and many moderately dysplastic dogs will lead normal lives if properly managed. A dysplastic dog should be kept in good weight and physical condition. Moderate exercise, especially swimming, is necessary if a dysplastic dog is to lead a normal life. If pain develops with age, it can be relieved with aspirin.

Another common condition that causes lameness in young dogs is **osteochondritis dissecans (OCD).** This disease affects the shoulder joints and sometimes the hocks and stifles. It is caused by faulty cartilage lining the ends of the long bones. As a dog exercises, either normally or under abnormal stress, the cartilage is damaged. OCD can be confirmed by X-ray, and the cartilage appears fragmented or loose. In mild cases it will heal itself with rest but usually requires surgery.

Another serious concern with lameness, especially as a dog ages, is **bone cancer.** This can only be confirmed by tests and X-rays. Anytime a dog or puppy becomes lame and rest is prescribed as treatment, it is essential to keep that dog almost completely inactive except for potty visits until the injury heals. A "little" walk will only prolong the recuperation. It can be difficult to confine extremely active dogs and keep them from reinjuring

themselves. Often it is necessary to keep these dogs in crates in order for them to heal.

Not Eating or Vomiting

One of the surest signs that a Golden Retriever may be ill is if it does not eat. This is why it is important to know your dog's eating habits. For most dogs one missed meal under normal conditions is not cause for alarm, but more than that and it is time to search for reasons. The vital signs should be checked and gums examined. Normally a dog's gums are pink; if ill they will be pale and gray.

If a lack of appetite has no other associated symptoms, it may be a sign of some form of cancer. Blood work done by a veterinarian is necessary for diagnosis. Poor appetite is also associated with kidney failure. Another indication that this may be occurring is increased water consumption and frequent urination. Dogs with kidney failure need special medication, an appetite booster and a special diet. An unspayed female with poor appetite and signs of lethargy may have pyometra, an infection of the uterus.

A healthy Golden will go all day.

There are many reasons why dogs vomit, and many of them are not cause for alarm. If they eat too much grass they vomit. If they drink too much water too fast they often vomit. If they eat something that does not agree with them they get rid of it before it makes them more ill. If no other vomiting occurs no action needs to be taken other than giving Kaopectate or Pepto Bismol and feeding the dog a mild diet for a day or so.

You should be concerned when your dog vomits frequently over the period of a day. If the vomiting is associated with diarrhea, elevated temperature and lethargy, the cause is most likely a virus. The dog should receive supportive veterinary treatment if recovery is to proceed quickly.

Vomiting that is not associated with other symptoms is often an indication of an intestinal blockage. Considering the oral orientations of most Golden Retrievers this can be a real concern. Rocks, toys and clothing will lodge in a dog's intestine, preventing the normal passage of digested foods and liquids. This is often difficult for a veterinarian to diagnose. Many times they will treat blockages as gastrointestinal disturbances for days until the dog becomes so weakened and dehydrated it dies.

If a blockage is suspected the first thing to do is an X-ray of the stomach and intestinal region. Sometimes objects will pass on their own, but usually surgical removal of the object is necessary.

Diarrhea

Diarrhea is characterized as very loose to watery stools that a dog has difficulty controlling. It can be caused by anything as simple as changing diet, eating rich human food or having internal parasites.

First try to locate the source of the problem and remove it from the dog's access. Immediate relief is usually available by giving the dog a human intestinal relief medication such as Kaopectate or Pepto Bismol. Use the same amount per weight as for humans. Take the dog off its food for a day to allow the

---

IDENTIFYING YOUR DOG

It's a terrible thing to think about, but your dog could somehow, someday, get lost or stolen. How would you get him back? Your best bet would be to have some form of identification on your dog. You can choose from a collar and tags, a tattoo, a microchip or a combination of these three.

Every dog should wear a buckle collar with identification tags. They are the quickest and easiest way for a stranger to identify your dog. It's best to inscribe the tags with your name and phone number; you don't need to include your dog's name.

There are two ways to permanently identify your dog. The first is a tattoo, placed on the inside of your dog's thigh. The tattoo should be your social security number or your dog's AKC registration number.

The second is a microchip, a rice-sized pellet that's inserted under the dog's skin at the base of the neck, between the shoulder blades. When a scanner is passed over the dog, it will beep, notifying the person that the dog has a chip. The scanner will then show a code, identifying the dog. Microchips are becoming more and more popular and are certainly the wave of the future.

intestines to rest, then feed meals of cooked rice with bland ingredients added. Gradually add the dog's regular food back into its diet.

If worms are suspected as the cause, a stool sample should be examined by a veterinarian and treatment to rid the dog of the parasite should follow when the dog is back to normal. If allergies are suspected, a series of tests can be given to find the cause. This is especially likely if, after recovery and no other evidence of a cause exists, a dog returns to its former diet and the diarrhea reccurs. If the diarrhea is bloody or has a more offensive odor than might be expected and is combined with vomiting and fever, it is most likely a virus and requires immediate veterinary attention.

Bloat

Another problem associated with the gastrointestinal system is bloat, or acute gastric dilatation. It most commonly occurs in adult dogs that eat large amounts of dry kibble. Exercise or excessive amounts of water consumed immediately following a meal can trigger the condition.

A dog with bloat will appear restless and uncomfortable. It may drool and attempt to vomit. The abdominal area will appear swollen, and the area will be painful. In severe cases the stomach actually twists on itself and a condition called torsion occurs.

The quickest way to provide relief as well as determine that it is gastric dilatation and not the more serious torsion (where the stomach twists 180 degrees on its own axis; volvulus is when the stomach rotates more than 180 degrees) is to insert a long rubber hose into the stomach; as the tube enters the stomach, there is a rush of air, bringing immediate relief.

In order to pass a stomach tube, first measure a length of tubing from the tip of the dog's nose to the last rib, then mark the tubing. Insert it behind one of the canine teeth and advance it into the throat until the dog begins to swallow. If the dog gags, continue to advance the tube. If the dog coughs, withdraw the tube and try again. There is small danger of damaging the esophagus with a soft rubber or plastic tube.

If the stomach has actually rotated, the tube cannot pass into it and your dog is in extreme danger. You have about 45 minutes to get it to a veterinarian with any hope of saving it. The torsion must be surgically corrected. New techniques in recent years have led many veterinarians to "tack" the stomach to the ribs in order to prevent future torsions.

If torsion has occurred, a dog will go into shock due to the lack of blood supply to the stomach and spleen.

Bloat can be prevented by feeding smaller amounts of food several times per day rather than in one large meal. Water can be withheld from the dog following a meal. Soaking the food in water prior to feeding it may also help reduce the risk of bloat. Additionally, the dog should be kept from exercising until two or three hours after eating.

Seizures

Seizures are one of the most frightening occurrences a dog owner can witness. Seizures vary in severity from trembling and stiffness to frenzied, rapid movements of the legs, foaming at the mouth and loss of urine and bowel movements. The latter is usually considered a grand mal seizure.

Seizures are caused by electrical activity in the brain, and there are many reasons why they may occur. Ingestion of some poisons, such as strychnine and insecticides, will cause seizures. These are generally long lasting and severe in nature. Blood work done often confirms the presence of poison and organ damage. Injuries to the skull, tumors and cancers can trigger seizures. Diagnosis of the injury or presence of the disease is usually enough to confirm the cause.

If there appears to be no reason for the seizure it is possible the cause is congenital epilepsy. This is particularly true if a dog is under the age of three. From the age of five, dogs are prone to develop old age onset epilepsy, which may have a genetic predisposition.

Seizures vary in length, and always seem longer than they actually are. Most first-time seizures that are not caused by poisonings will have a duration of up to two minutes. Typically the seizure will stop, and after a few minutes or even hours of disorientation, the dog returns to its normal behavior. Never try to touch or move a dog during a seizure. They may accidentally bite in this state. If there is anything nearby that might be knocked over by their flailing legs and injure them, move it out of the way. If the seizure does not stop within five minutes, call your veterinarian.

Even after a typical seizure, you may want to contact your veterinarian and discuss your options. Your vet may suggest you bring your dog in for an examination and blood work. If a cause is not found, the best course is usually to wait and see if your dog has another seizure. If a dog only seizures once or twice a year there is no reason to place it on preventive medication. If seizures occur on a regular basis and are of the same nature each time, the dog is considered to have epilepsy and medication should be started. Commonly used drugs to prevent seizures include phenobarbital and dilantin. The amount given will vary according to how much is needed to control frequent seizures.

Applying abdominal thrusts can save a choking dog.

In typical epilepsy, a dog is in a state of aura for as long as a day before the seizure occurs. The dog may act restless and stare and bark at things that do not exist. The seizure itself lasts several minutes. A second seizure can be triggered by turning a light on or moving the dog as it is recovering.

If seizures are infrequent and mild, an epileptic dog can lead a fairly normal life. Owners will generally begin to see a pattern in the time of day and frequency the seizures occur, and can plan their dog's activities accordingly. Nonetheless, it is probably not a wise idea to subject a seizure-prone dog to excessive stress or exercise. The frequency and intensity of seizures often increases as time goes on, until the quality of the dog's life is questionable.

Coughing

Throughout the day most dogs will cough to get something out of their throats and it is usually ignored. If coughing persists, then it is time to look for causes. Sometimes it is nothing more than grass seeds or a collar that is too tight.

A common cause for a dry hacking cough is kennel cough, which is contagious and usually picked up through association with other dogs. A dog with kennel cough should receive veterinary attention and be placed on antibiotics and a cough suppressant. During treatment and recovery, the dog should be kept indoors and warm as much as possible. Kennel cough, if not cared for properly, can easily turn into pneumonia in cold conditions. Dogs should be isolated from other dogs until they have recovered.

An Elizabethan collar keeps your dog from licking a fresh wound.

Coughing can also be a sign of heart failure, especially in an older dog after it has been exercised. It may also indicate a heartworm infection. If this occurs regularly, consult your veterinarian.

Most changes in the breathing pattern of a healthy dog, such as rapid inhalations or panting, are caused by exercise, stress and heat. The breathing pattern should return to normal in a short period of time.

If a dog is having problems breathing and it is also accompanied by coughing or gagging, it may be a sign that an air passage is blocked. Check for an object lodged in your dog's throat. If you can't remove it yourself, use the Heimlich maneuver. Place your dog on its side and, using both hands palms down, apply quick thrusts to the abdomen just below the dog's last rib. If your dog won't lie down, grasp either side of the end of the rib cage and squeeze in short thrusts. Make a sharp enough movement to cause the air in the lungs to force the object out. If the cause cannot be found or removed, then professional help is needed.

Shallow breathing can be a result of an injury to the ribs or a lung problem. A wheezing noise that can be heard as a dog breathes is an indication of a serious problem. If other symptoms include a fever and lethargy, the problem may be associated with a lung disease. If there is no fever it may indicate heart disease or a lung tumor. The symptoms may indicate treatment for an infection, but an X-ray can confirm the presence of a growth or infection in the lungs.

Sometimes a dog exhibits no other signs that something is different than increased lethargy, weight gain and even a poor coat. It may be time to

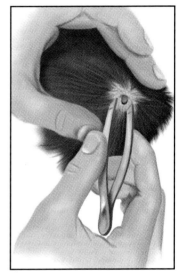

Use tweezers to remove ticks from your dog.

consider checking the dog's thyroid levels for a possible hypothyroid condition. Low thyroid most commonly results in a poor coat and skin and eventual infertility in an intact male or female. A thyroid test will indicate what levels of the function of the thyroid are low and whether daily thyroid medication should be given.

Skin Problems

Certain skin conditions should not be ignored if home treatment is not working. For example, if a dog is so sensitive and allergic to the saliva of a flea that its coat and skin are literally destroyed by chewing, it is time to seek help. Cortisone can help relieve the itching and stop the dog from destroying itself, but it has side effects, too! It's best to get your vet's advice.

Mange is caused by a tiny mite that lives on the dog's skin. The most common types are sarcoptic and demodetic mange. While they can be treated without veterinary assistance, actual diagnosis may have to be by a veterinarian as the mites are too small to be seen.

Sarcoptic mange first occurs as small red bumps on the dog's skin and causes intense itching. If allowed to continue there is hair loss from chewing, and the affected skin becomes crusty.

To give a pill, open the mouth wide, then drop it in the back of the throat.

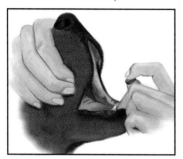

The mite that causes demodetic mange lives in the pores of the skin of most dogs. Certain conditions cause the dog's natural immunity to this mite to break down, and the result is patches of hair loss, usually around the nose or eyes. There is no itching associated with this condition and it primarily occurs in dogs under one year of age. If treated properly the hair returns to normal. In the generalized form of the disease, hair loss occurs in large patches all over the body. Obviously this is a much more serious condition.

One of the most baffling skin problems is **hot spots.** They can be caused by a number of things—flea bites and allergies being culprits. A warm, moist, infected area on the skin appears out of nowhere and can be several inches large. At home one should clip the hair around it, then clean it with an antiseptic cleaning solution and dilute hydrogen peroxide. Topical ointments can also help. If the spot is not healing and appears to be getting larger or infected, veterinary help should be sought.

A similar type of skin condition is the **lick sore.** These sores are almost always on the lower part of the front legs or tops of the feet. Some dogs are more prone to develop these than others. A dog will lick a spot and out of boredom continue licking it until the hair is gone and the skin is hard, red and shiny. The sore will heal on its own if kept clean and the dog is prevented access to it by an anti-chewing spray or by wearing an Elizabethan collar.

A condition that is not serious but frequently causes concern because it looks so strange is an **ear hematoma,** often termed pillow ear. Due to an infection or ear mite infestation, the dog shakes its head vigorously and bursts a blood vessel in the ear. The inside of the ear flap fills with blood until it is engorged. If left untreated the blood will eventually dry, but the ear is left deformed in shape. If treated by a veterinarian, he or she will put a drain in the ear flap to remove the blood and fluids until it has healed. The ear will return to normal if handled in this manner.

Tumors

As dogs age they are more apt to develop various types of tumors. These may be sebaceous cysts, which appear as small bumps on or within the skin. They are usually harmless unless they become infected and begin to increase in size. Fatty tumors grow just under the dog's skin and are not attached to anything. These are usually benign accumulations of fatty cells. If you see or feel any such lumps on your dog, you should consult your veterinarian. Tumors and bumps that appear and grow rapidly, are strange in color or appearance or are attached to the bone should receive immediate attention.

Giving Medication

Anytime a dog has been diagnosed with a problem that requires medication it is usually in the form of a pill or liquid.

Because it is essential for a dog to have the entire pill or capsule in order for the dosage to be effective, it's necessary to actually give the dog the pill rather than mixing it in his food or wrapping it in meat, which can

Squeeze eye ointment into the lower lid.

85

be chewed up and spit out. Open your dog's mouth and place the pill on the back of the middle of his tongue. Then hold his head up with his mouth held shut and stroke his throat. When the dog swallows, you can let go.

Liquid medication is most easily given in a syringe. These are usually marked so the amount is accurately measured. Hold the dog's head upward at about 45 degrees, open the mouth slightly and place the end of the syringe in the area in the back of the mouth between the cheek and rear molars. Hold your dog's mouth shut until he swallows.

If your dog needs eye medication, apply it by pulling down the lower eyelid and placing the ointment on the inside of the lid. Then close the eye and gently disperse the solution around the eye. Eye drops can be placed directly on the eye. Giving ear medicine is similar to cleaning the ears. The drops are placed in the canal and the ear is then massaged.

Run your hands regularly over your dog to feel for any injuries.

Cuts and Wounds

Lacerations of the skin most commonly occur from dog fights, though dogs have been known to do such things as go through a window after a cat or rabbit. Any cut over half an inch in length should be stitched for it to heal. Small cuts usually heal by themselves if they are rinsed well, washed with an antibiotic soap and checked regularly with further cleansing of soap or a hydrogen peroxide solution. When they occur in areas that are exposed to dirt, such as the feet, it may be advisable to place a wrap on the injury, but it should be removed frequently. If signs of infection appear, such as swelling, redness and warmth, it should be looked at by a veterinarian.

Puncture wounds should never be bandaged or stitched. They occur most commonly from bites, nails or wires. Anytime it is suspected that a dog might have been pierced by a nail or bitten, the body should be carefully examined for such wounds. As they often do not bleed very much they can be difficult to spot. If not treated, they can result in infection or even conditions as dangerous as tetanus.

If the wound is discovered within a short time of the occurrence, try to make it bleed by applying pressure around it. Flush it with water, then clean it with soap. Leave it exposed so that oxygen is able to stay in the wound and prevent an anaerobic condition from developing. Place a dilute hydrogen peroxide on it several times a day. Watch it carefully for any indications of infection. Anytime your dog is injured, consider placing her on an antibiotic to prevent infection.

If you know your dog, you'll probably know when something's wrong.

Common Golden Retriever Problems

Cataracts: There are several types of cataracts that affect Goldens. They are characterized by the part of the lens on which they appear and the age of the dog. Most are genetic, though others can be caused by injury or the aging process. Most cataracts are non-progressive in Goldens and impairment of vision is usually mild. Diagnosis must be made by a veterinary ophthalmologist.

Epilepsy: Genetic epilepsy usually appears prior to three years of age. The old age onset form may have a genetic predisposition. These are seizures that occur regularly and follow a typical pattern. Epilepsy can be controlled by daily medication.

Hip dysplasia: Genetic and environmental in origin, it is the malformation of the ball and socket joints of the hips. Severe forms cause lameness and may require surgery. Diagnosis is only by X-ray.

Low Thyroid *(Hypothyroidism):* It may be genetic and is also associated with poor immunity. There may be physical signs such as weight gain, lethargy, poor coat, infertility in both sexes and longer than normal periods of time between heat cycles. A thyroid test will indicate if there is a problem. Daily medication will correct the thyroid levels and return a dog to normal.

Use a scarf or old hose to make a temporary muzzle, as shown.

Lymphosarcoma: This form of cancer, which affects the lymph system, is becoming alarmingly common in many related and unrelated families of Goldens. Symptoms may include poor appetite, lethargy and always swollen lymph nodes. Treatment can prolong a dog's life for as much as a year. Dogs may be genetically predisposed to it, and it is linked to autoimmune problems.

Osteochondritis dissecans *(OCD):* There appears to be a genetic predisposition to malformation of the cartilage of the long bones that subsequently results in the injury of that cartilage. This can be treated by rest in minor cases or surgery. X-rays verify this condition.

Progressive Retinal Atrophy *(PRA):* This is less common in Goldens than cataracts, but it still occurs. PRA is a gradual degeneration of the cells of the retina. It first occurs in middle-aged dogs and leads to loss of vision. Diagnosis is the same as for cataracts. CERF (the Canine Eye Registry Foundation) was established to register dogs whose eyes test free of genetic problems to benefit breeding programs.

Skin Allergies and Hot Spots: A genetic predisposition to skin allergies may exist. The thick undercoat, especially if it stays damp, is an excellent environment for the development of hot spots.

Subaortic Stenosis *(SAS):* This is a genetically caused defect in the valve ring below the aorta of the heart. It is detected by a murmur, and accurate diagnosis is made by a variety of advanced techniques including auscultation and echo-cardiogram. In cases of minor murmurs a dog should lead a normal though sedate life. Dogs with severe grades of SAS will show physical signs and often die unexpectedly at a young age. Diagnosis should be made by a registered canine cardiologist.

von Willebrands Disease: A genetic bleeding disorder that might be suspected if it takes longer than normal for a wound to stop bleeding. Other indications are high mortality rates in newborn puppies or poor fertility in a female. A blood specimen treated and tested at a specially equipped facility is necessary to diagnose this disease.

In the case of life-threatening injuries or illnesses a dog owner often faces a dilemma in just getting the animal to a clinic for treatment. Ambulance service for animals is nonexistent and in some areas finding a veterinarian who is open at odd hours and days is difficult.

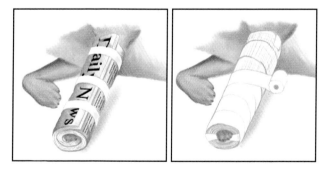

Make a temporary splint by wrapping the leg in firm casing, then bandaging it.

Often they are available, but many miles away. While we never plan on emergencies happening we can be partially prepared by knowing which veterinary clinics are open if something occurs at night or on the weekend. Telephone numbers should be posted so they can be

Living with a
Golden
Retriever

easily located. As businesses often change, update this information periodically for accuracy.

First Aid and Emergencies

So far we have discussed various symptoms, what they might indicate and when veterinary treatment should be sought. First-aid measures can be taken to help ensure that your dog gets to a veterinarian in time for treatment to be effective.

Anytime a dog is in extreme pain, even the most docile one may bite if touched. As a precaution, the dog's mouth should be restrained with some type of **muzzle.** A rope, pair of pantyhose or strip of cloth about two feet long all work in a pinch.

First tie a loose knot that has an opening large enough to easily fit around the dog's nose. Once it is on, tighten the knot on the top of the muzzle. Then bring the two ends down and tie another knot underneath the dog's chin. Finally, pull the ends behind the head and tie a knot below the ears. Don't do this if there is an injury to the head or the dog requires artificial respiration.

Artificial respiration is necessary if breathing has stopped. Situations that may cause a state of unconsciousness include drowning, choking, electric shock or even shock itself. If you've taken a course in human CPR you will discover that similar methods are used on dogs. The first thing to do is check the mouth

A FIRST-AID KIT

Keep a canine first-aid kit on hand for general care and emergencies. Check it periodically to make sure liquids haven't spilled or dried up, and replace medications and materials after they're used. Your kit should include:

Activated charcoal tablets

Adhesive tape
(1 and 2 inches wide)

Antibacterial ointment
(for skin and eyes)

Aspirin (buffered or enteric coated, *not* Ibuprofen)

Bandages: Gauze rolls (1 and 2 inches wide) and dressing pads

Cotton balls

Diarrhea medicine

Dosing syringe

Hydrogen peroxide (3%)

Petroleum jelly

Rectal thermometer

Rubber gloves

Rubbing alcohol

Scissors

Tourniquet

Towel

Tweezers

90

and air passages for any object that might obstruct breathing. If you find nothing, or when it is cleared, hold the dog's mouth while covering the nose completely with your mouth. Gently exhale into the dog's nose. This should be done at between ten to twelve breaths per minute.

If the heart has stopped beating, place the dog on its right side and place the palm of your hand on the rib cage just behind the elbows. Press down six times and then wait five seconds and repeat. This should be done in conjunction with artificial respiration, so it will require two people. Artificial respiration should be continued until the dog breathes on its own or the heart beats. Heart massage should continue until the heart beats on its own or no beat is felt for five minutes.

Some of the many household substances harmful to your dog.

If a dog has been injured or is too ill to walk on its own it will have to carried to be moved. It is important to be very careful when this is done to prevent further injury or trauma. Keep the dog's body as flat and still as possible. Two people are usually needed to move a large dog. A blanket can work if all four corners are held taut. A piece of plywood or extremely stiff cardboard works best, if available.

Whenever a dog is injured or is seriously ill the odds are good that it will go into a state of **shock.** A dog in shock will be listless, weak and cold to the touch. Its gums will be pale. If not treated a dog will die from shock even if the illness or injuries themselves are not fatal. The conditions of the dog should continue to be treated, but the dog should be kept as comfortable as possible. A blanket can help keep the dog warm. A dog in shock needs immediate veterinary care.

When **severe bleeding** from a cut occurs the area should be covered with bandaging material or a clean cloth and should have pressure applied to it. If it appears that an artery is involved and the wound is on a limb, then a tourniquet should be applied. This can be made of a piece of cloth, gauze or sock if nothing else is available. It should be tied above the wound and checked every few minutes to make sure it is not so tight that circulation to the rest of the limb is cut off.

If a **fracture** is felt or suspected, the dog should be moved and transported as carefully as possible to a veterinarian. Attempting to treat a break at home can cause more damage than leaving it alone.

In the case of **poisoning** the only thing to do is get help immediately. If you know the source of the poison, take the container or object with you as this may aid treatment. If a dog ingests a petroleum product, vegetable or mineral oil can be given for the gastrointestinal tract at a dosage of one tablespoon per five pounds of weight.

In acidic or alkaline poisonings the chemicals must be neutralized. Pepto Bismol or milk of magnesia at two teaspoons per five pounds can be given for acids. Vinegar diluted at one part to four parts water at the same dosage can relieve alkaline poisons.

Heatstroke

Heatstroke occurs when a dog's body temperature greatly exceeds the normal 102.5 degrees. It can be caused by overexercise in warm temperatures, or if a dog is left in a closed vehicle for any period of time. A dog should *never* be left in an unventilated, unshaded vehicle. Even if you only plan to be gone for a minute, that time can unexpectedly increase and place a dog in a life-threatening situation.

Dogs suffering from heatstroke will feel hot to the touch and inhale short, shallow, rapid breaths. The heartbeat will be very fast. The dog must be cooled immediately, preferably being wet down with cool water in any way that is available. The dog should be wrapped in cool, damp towels. Shock is another possible side effect of heatstroke. The dog should also receive veterinary care. Even when a dog survives heatstroke, permanent damage often occurs.

The opposite of heatstroke is **hypothermia.** When a dog is exposed to extreme cold for long periods of time its body temperature drops, it becomes chilled and it can go into shock. The dog should be placed in a warm environment and wrapped in towels or blankets. If the dog is already wet, a warm bath can help. Massaging the body will help increase the circulation to normal levels.

Insect Bites

The seriousness of reactions to insect bites varies. The affected area will be red, swollen and painful. In the case of bee stings the stinger should always be removed. A paste made of baking soda can be applied to the wound and ice applied to the area for the relief of swelling. The bites of some spiders, centipedes and scorpions can cause severe illness and lead to shock.

Poisonous snakebites are much more serious. They are not only very painful but the dog will often go into a state of panic. Apply a tourniquet above the area of the bite to help stop the flow of venom to the body. Parallel incisions should be made through the area of the wound and then the blood sucked out. The blood must be spit out and it should not be done if you have a wound in your mouth. A suction device is preferable to your mouth, if it is available. This should be continued for up to thirty minutes. Periodically loosen the tourniquet. The dog should receive veterinary attention immediately.

Porcupines

If a dog has an encounter with a porcupine, those quills will need to be removed. The quill should be grasped with a pair of pliers in the area just above the dog's skin. A quick tug should remove it. If a quill breaks off and is left in the skin it will need to be removed by a veterinarian. If left in, the quills can migrate through the dog's body and cause infection.

Skunks

If your dog is sprayed by a skunk he will not require veterinary attention, but he will be unbearable to live with. Getting rid of the odor is not easy, despite all of the remedies in the world. Several products are available specifically for skunk-odor removal. If you can't find or buy one in time, plain old vinegar can work, as can mixtures of baking soda and hydrogen peroxide, or good old tomato juice. Some people find feminine douche preparations effective.

Despite what one decides to use the dog will need to be thoroughly wet down. The solution is then applied to the dog's coat and allowed to sit for ten minutes (or whatever the directions recommend). Even after being rinsed off with clear water the odor often remains. Repeating the process several times is often necessary. A faint skunk odor may linger for some time even after the most thorough de-skunking sessions.

Foxtails

Of all the things on this earth that plague man and dog, possibly the worst is the foxtail, a kind of burr from a plant. Foxtails are barbed awns with a sharp point that are usually found in wheat-growing areas. This pest is very lightweight and is easily inhaled by the dog or lodged in its ear or eye. It's barbed enough to cling to rear or belly hair, from where it then makes its way into the anus, vaginal or penile sheath. That in itself is bad enough, but this terrible object keeps moving forward under the skin and into your dog's system. It has been known to travel to the heart and kill a dog. The only means of prevention is to keep the dog away from open fields.

If that's not possible, you can use a vegetable oil, cooking spray, creme rinse, or similar product on your dog's feet, around the anus, the ears, eyes, nose, lips and chest—any place the foxtail is likely to lodge. The foxtail cannot stick to such a slippery surface and, though it may cling to the hairs, it is easily removed.

Your Happy, Healthy Pet

Your Dog's Name _____

Name on Your Dog's Pedigree (if your dog has one) _____

_____

Where Your Dog Came From _____

_____

Your Dog's Birthday _____

Your Dog's Veterinarian

    Name   _____

    Address   _____

    Phone Number_____

    Emergency Number_____

Your Dog's Health

    Vaccines

    type _____ date given _____

    type _____ date given _____

    type _____ date given _____

    type _____ date given _____

    Heartworm

    date tested _____ type used_____ start date _____

Your Dog's License Number_____

Groomer's Name and Number _____

Dogsitter/Walker's Name and Number _____

Awards Your Dog Has Won

    Award _____ date earned _____

    Award _____ date earned _____

part three

Enjoying your Dog

chapter 8

Basic
Training

by Ian Dunbar, Ph.D., MRCVS

Training is the jewel in the crown—the most important aspect of doggy husbandry. There is no more important variable influencing dog behavior and temperament than the dog's education: A well-trained, well-behaved and good-natured puppydog is always a joy to live with, but an untrained and uncivilized dog can be a perpetual nightmare. Moreover, deny the dog an education and it will not have the opportunity to fulfill its own canine potential; neither will it have the ability to communicate effectively with its human companions.

Luckily, modern psychological training methods are easy, efficient and effective and, above all, considerably dog-friendly and user-friendly. Doggy education is as simple as it is enjoyable. But before you can have a good time play-training with your new dog, you have to learn what to do and how to do it. There is no bigger variable influencing the success of dog training than the *owner's* experience and expertise. *Before you embark on the dog's education, you must first educate yourself.*

Basic Training for Owners

Ideally, basic owner training should begin well *before* you select your dog. Find out all you can about your chosen breed first, then master rudimentary training and handling skills. If you already have your puppy/dog, owner training is a dire emergency—the clock is running! Especially for puppies, the first few weeks at home are the most important and influential days in the dog's life. Indeed, the cause of most adolescent and adult problems may be traced back to the initial days the pup explores his new home. This is the time to establish the *status quo*—to teach the puppy/dog how you would like him to behave and so prevent otherwise quite predictable problems.

In addition to consulting breeders and breed books such as this one (which understandably have a positive breed bias), seek out as many pet owners with your breed you can find. Good points are obvious. What you want to find out are the breed-specific *problems*, so you can nip them in the bud. In particular, you should talk to owners with *adolescent* dogs and make a list of all anticipated problems. Most important, *test drive* at least half a dozen adolescent and adult dogs of your breed yourself. An eight-week-old puppy is deceptively easy to handle, but she will acquire adult size, speed and strength in just four months, so you should learn now what to prepare for.

Puppy and pet dog training classes offer a convenient venue to locate pet owners and observe dogs in action. For a list of suitable trainers in your area, contact the Association of Pet Dog Trainers (see Chapter 13). You may also begin your basic owner training by observing other owners in class. Watch as many classes and test drive as many dogs as possible. Select an upbeat, dog-friendly, people-friendly, fun-and-games, puppydog pet training class to learn the ropes. Also, watch training videos and read training books (see Chapter 12). You must find out what to do and how to do it *before* you have to do it.

Principles of Training

Most people think training comprises teaching the dog to do things such as sit, speak and roll over, but even a four-week-old pup knows how to do these things already. Instead, the first step in training involves teaching the dog human words for each dog behavior and activity and for each aspect of the dog's environment. That way you, the owner, can more easily participate in the dog's domestic education by directing him to perform specific actions appropriately, that is, at the right time, in the right place, and so on. Training opens communication channels, enabling an educated dog to at least understand the owner's requests.

In addition to teaching a dog *what* we want her to do, it is also necessary to teach her *why* she should do what we ask. Indeed, 95 percent of training revolves around motivating the dog *to want to do* what we want. Dogs often understand what their owners want; they just don't see the point of doing it—especially when the owner's repetitively boring and seemingly senseless instructions are totally at odds with much more pressing and exciting doggy distractions. It is not so much the dog who is being stubborn or dominant; rather, it is the owner who has failed to acknowledge the dog's needs and feelings and to approach training from the dog's point of view.

The Meaning of Instructions

The secret to successful training is learning how to use training lures to predict or prompt specific behaviors—to coax the dog to do what you want *when* you want. Any highly valued object (such as a treat or toy) may be used as a lure, which the dog will follow with his eyes and nose. Moving the lure in specific ways entices the dog to move his nose, head and entire body in specific ways. In fact, by learning the art of manipulating various lures, it is possible to teach the dog to assume virtually any body position and perform any action. Once you have control over the expression of the dog's behaviors and can elicit any body position or behavior at will, you can easily teach the dog to perform on request.

Tell your dog what you want him to do, use a lure to entice him to respond correctly, then profusely praise

Teach your dog words for each activity he needs to know, like down.

and maybe reward him once he performs the desired action. For example, verbally request "Fido, sit!" while you move a squeaky toy upwards and backwards over the dog's muzzle (lure-movement and hand signal), smile knowingly as he looks up (to follow the lure) and sits down (as a result of canine anatomical engineering), then praise him to distraction ("Goood Fido!"). Squeak the toy, offer a training treat and give your dog and yourself a pat on the back.

Being able to elicit desired responses over and over enables the owner to reward the dog over and over. Consequently, the dog begins to think training is fun. For example, the more the dog is rewarded for sitting, the more she enjoys sitting. Eventually the dog comes to realize that, whereas most sitting is appreciated, sitting immediately upon request usually prompts especially enthusiastic praise and a slew of high-level rewards. The dog begins to sit on cue much of the time, showing that she is starting to grasp the meaning of the owner's verbal request and hand signal.

Why Comply?

Most dogs enjoy initial lure/reward training and are only too happy to comply with their owners' wishes. Unfortunately, repetitive drilling without appreciative feedback tends to diminish the dog's enthusiasm until he eventually fails to see the point of complying anymore. Moreover, as the dog approaches adolescence he becomes more easily distracted as he develops other interests. Lengthy sessions with repetitive exercises tend to bore and demotivate both parties. If it's not fun, the owner doesn't do it and neither does the dog.

Integrate training into your dog's life: The greater number of training sessions each day and the *shorter* they are, the more willingly compliant your dog will become. Make sure to have a short (just a few seconds) training interlude before every enjoyable canine activity. For example, ask your dog to sit to greet people, to sit before you throw his Frisbee, and to sit for his supper. Really, sitting is no different from a canine "please." Also, include numerous short training interludes during every enjoyable canine pastime, for example, when playing with the dog or when he is running in the park. In this fashion, doggy distractions may be effectively converted into rewards for training. Just as all games have rules, fun becomes training . . . and training becomes fun.

Eventually, rewards actually become unnecessary to continue motivating your dog. If trained with consideration and kindness, performing the desired behaviors will become self-rewarding and, in a sense, your dog will motivate himself. Just as it is not necessary to reward a human companion during an enjoyable walk in the park, or following a game of tennis, it is hardly necessary to reward our best friend—the dog—for walking by our side or while playing fetch. Human

company during enjoyable activities is reward enough for most dogs.

Even though your dog has become self-motivating, it's still good to praise and pet him a lot and offer rewards once in a while, especially for a good job well done. And if for no other reason, praising and rewarding others is good for the human heart.

To train your dog, you need gentle hands, a loving heart and a good attitude.

Punishment

Without a doubt, lure/reward training is by far the best way to teach: Entice your dog to do what you want and then reward him for doing so. Unfortunately, a human shortcoming is to take the good for granted and to moan and groan at the bad. Specifically, the dog's many good behaviors are ignored while the owner focuses on punishing the dog for making mistakes. In extreme cases, instruction is *limited* to punishing mistakes made by a trainee dog, child, employee or husband, even though it has been proven punishment training is notoriously inefficient and ineffective and is decidedly unfriendly and combative. It teaches the dog that training is a drag, almost as quickly as it teaches the dog to dislike his trainer. Why treat our best friends like our worst enemies?

Punishment training is also much more laborious and time consuming. Whereas it takes only a finite amount of time to teach a dog what to chew, for example, it takes much, much longer to punish the dog for each and every mistake. Remember, *there is only one right way!* So why not teach that right way from the outset?!

To make matters worse, punishment training causes severe lapses in the dog's reliability. Since it is obviously impossible to punish the dog each and every time she misbehaves, the dog quickly learns to distinguish between those times when she must comply (so as to avoid impending punishment) and those times when she need not comply, because punishment is impossible. Such times include when the dog is off leash and only six feet away, when the owner is otherwise engaged (talking to a friend, watching television, taking a shower, tending to the baby or chatting on the telephone), or when the dog is left at home alone.

Instances of misbehavior will be numerous when the owner is away, because even when the dog complied in the owner's looming presence, he did so unwillingly. The dog was forced to act against his will, rather than moulding his will to want to please. Hence, when the owner is absent, not only does the dog know he need not comply, he simply does not want to. Again, the trainee is not a stubborn vindictive beast, but rather the trainer has failed to teach.

Punishment training invariably creates unpredictable Jekyll and Hyde behavior.

Trainer's Tools

Many training books extol the virtues of a vast array of training paraphernalia and electronic and metallic gizmos, most of which are designed for canine restraint, correction and punishment, rather than for actual facilitation of doggy education. In reality, most effective training tools are not found in stores; they come from within ourselves. In addition to a willing dog, all you really need is a functional human brain, gentle hands, a loving heart and a good attitude.

In terms of equipment, all dogs do require a quality buckle collar to sport dog tags and to attach the leash (for safety and to comply with local leash laws). Hollow chewtoys (like Kongs or sterilized longbones) and a dog bed or collapsible crate are a must for housetraining. Three additional tools are required:

1. specific lures (training treats and toys) to predict and prompt specific desired behaviors;

2. rewards (praise, affection, training treats and toys) to reinforce for the dog what a lot of fun it all is; and

3. knowledge—how to convert the dog's favorite activities and games (potential distractions to training) into "life-rewards," which may be employed to facilitate training.

The most powerful of these is *knowledge*. Education is the key! Watch training classes, participate in training classes, watch videos, read books, enjoy playtraining with your dog, and then your dog will say "Please," and your dog will say "Thank you!"

Housetraining

If dogs were left to their own devices, certainly they would chew, dig and bark for entertainment and then no doubt highlight a few areas of their living space with sprinkles of urine, in much the same way we decorate by hanging pictures. Consequently, when we ask a dog to live with us, we must teach him *where* he may dig and perform his toilet duties, *what* he may chew and *when* he may bark. After all, when left at home alone for many hours, we cannot expect the dog to amuse himself by completing crosswords or watching the soaps on TV!

Also, it would be decidedly unfair to keep the house rules a secret from the dog, and then get angry and punish the poor critter for inevitably transgressing rules he did not even know existed. Remember, without adequate education and guidance, the dog will be forced to establish his own rules—doggy rules—that most probably will be at odds with the owner's view of domestic living.

Since most problems develop during the first few days the dog is at home, prospective dog owners must be certain they are quite clear about the principles of housetraining *before* they get a dog. Early misbehaviors quickly become established as the status quo—

becoming firmly entrenched as hard-to-break bad habits, which set the precedent for years to come. Make sure to teach your dog good habits right from the start. Good habits are just as hard to break as bad ones!

Ideally, when a new dog comes home, try to arrange for someone to be present for as much as possible during the first few days (for adult dogs) or weeks for puppies. With only a little forethought, it is surprisingly easy to find a puppy sitter, such as a retired person, who would be willing to eat from your refrigerator and watch your television while keeping an eye on the newcomer to encourage the dog to play with chewtoys and to ensure he goes outside on a regular basis.

POTTY TRAINING

To teach the dog where to relieve himself:

1. never let him make a single mistake;

2. let him know where you want him to go; and

3. handsomely reward him for doing so: "GOOOOOOOD DOG!!!" liver treat, liver treat, liver treat!

PREVENTING MISTAKES

A single mistake is a training disaster, since it heralds many more in future weeks. And each time the dog soils the house, this further reinforces the dog's unfortunate preference for an indoor, carpeted toilet. *Do not let an unhousetrained dog have full run of the house if you are away from home or cannot pay full attention.* Instead, confine the dog to an area where elimination is appropriate, such as an outdoor run or, better still, a small, comfortable indoor kennel with access to an outdoor run. When confined in this manner, most dogs will naturally housetrain themselves.

If that's not possible, confine the dog to an area, such as a utility room, kitchen, basement or garage, where elimination may not be desired in the long run but as an interim measure it is certainly preferable to doing it all around the house. Use newspaper to cover the floor of the dog's day room. The newspaper may be used to soak up the urine and to wrap up and dispose of the feces. Once your dog develops a preferred spot for eliminating, it is only necessary to cover that part of the floor with newspaper. The smaller papered area may then be moved (only a little each day) towards the door to the outside. Thus the dog will develop the tendency to go to the door when he needs to relieve himself.

Never confine an unhousetrained dog to a crate for long periods. Doing so would force the dog to soil the crate and ruin its usefulness as an aid for housetraining (see the following discussion).

The first few weeks at home are the most important and influential in your dog's life.

TEACHING WHERE

In order to teach your dog where you would like her to do her business, you have to be there to direct the proceedings—an obvious, yet often neglected, fact of life. In order to be there to teach the dog *where* to go, you need to know *when* she needs to go. Indeed, the success of housetraining depends on the owner's ability to predict these times. Certainly, a regular feeding schedule will facilitate prediction somewhat, but there is nothing like "loading the deck" and influencing the timing of the outcome yourself!

Whenever you are at home, make sure the dog is under constant supervision and/or confined to a small area. If already well trained, simply instruct the dog to lie down in his bed or basket. Alternatively, confine the dog to a crate (doggy den) or tie-down (a short, 18-inch lead that can be clipped to an eye hook in the baseboard). Short-term close confinement strongly inhibits urination and defecation, since the dog does not want to soil his sleeping area. Thus, when you release the puppydog each hour, he will definitely need to urinate immediately and defecate every third or fourth hour. Keep the dog confined to his doggy den and take him to his intended toilet area each hour, every hour, and on the hour.

When taking your dog outside, instruct him to sit quietly before opening the door—he will soon learn to sit by the door when he needs to go out!

TEACHING WHY

Being able to predict when the dog needs to go enables the owner to be on the spot to praise and reward the dog. Each hour, hurry the dog to the intended toilet area in the yard, issue the appropriate instruction ("Go pee!" or "Go poop!"), then give the dog three to four minutes to produce. Praise and offer a couple of training treats when successful. The treats are important because many people fail to praise their dogs with feeling . . . and housetraining is hardly the time for understatement. So either loosen up and enthusiastically praise that dog: "Wuzzzer-wuzzer-wuzzer, hoooser good wuffer den? Hoooo went pee for Daddy?" Or say "Good dog!" as best you can and offer the treats for effect.

Following elimination is an ideal time for a spot of playtraining in the yard or house. Also, an empty dog may be allowed greater freedom around the house for the next half hour or so, just as long as you keep an eye out to make sure he does not get into other kinds of mischief. If you are preoccupied and cannot pay full attention, confine the dog to his doggy den once more to enjoy a peaceful snooze or to play with his many chewtoys.

If your dog does not eliminate within the allotted time outside—no biggie! Back to his doggy den, and then try again after another hour.

As I own large dogs, I always feel more relaxed walking an empty dog, knowing that I will not need to finish our stroll weighted down with bags of feces! Beware of falling into the trap of walking the dog to get it to eliminate. The good ol' dog walk is such an enormous highlight in the dog's life that it represents the single biggest potential reward in domestic dogdom. However, when in a hurry, or during inclement weather, many owners abruptly terminate the walk the moment the dog has done its business. This, in effect, severely punishes the dog for doing the right thing, in the right place at the right time. Consequently, many dogs become strongly inhibited from eliminating outdoors because they know it will signal an abrupt end to an otherwise thoroughly enjoyable walk.

Instead, instruct the dog to relieve himself in the yard prior to going for a walk. If you follow the above instructions, most dogs soon learn to eliminate on cue. As soon as the dog eliminates, praise (and offer a treat or two)—"Good dog! Let's go walkies!" Use the walk as a reward for eliminating in the yard. If the dog does not go, put him back in his doggy den and think about a walk later on. You will find with a "No feces–no walk" policy, your dog will become one of the fastest defecators in the business.

If you do not have a back yard, instruct the dog to eliminate right outside your front door prior to the walk. Not only will this facilitate clean up and disposal of the feces in your own trash can but, also, the walk may again be used as a colossal reward.

CHEWING AND BARKING

Short-term close confinement also teaches the dog that occasional quiet moments are a reality of domestic living. Your puppydog is extremely impressionable during his first few weeks at home. Regular confinement at this time soon exerts a calming influence over the dog's personality. Remember, once the dog is housetrained and calmer, there will be a whole lifetime ahead for the dog to enjoy full run of the house and garden. On the other hand, by letting the newcomer have unrestricted access to the entire household and allowing him to run willy-nilly, he will most certainly develop a bunch of behavior problems in short order, no doubt necessitating confinement later in life. It would not be fair to remedially restrain and confine a dog you have trained, through neglect, to run free.

When confining the dog, make sure he always has an impressive array of suitable chewtoys. Kongs and sterilized longbones (both readily available from pet stores) make the best chewtoys, since they are hollow and may be stuffed with treats to heighten the dog's interest. For example, by stuffing the little hole at the top of a Kong with a small piece of freeze-dried liver, the dog will not want to leave it alone.

Remember, treats do not have to be junk food and they certainly should not represent extra calories. Rather, treats should be part of each dog's regular daily diet:

Make sure your puppy has suitable chewtoys.

Some food may be served in the dog's bowl for breakfast and dinner, some food may be used as training treats, and some food may be used for stuffing chewtoys. I regularly stuff my dogs' many Kongs with different shaped biscuits and kibble. The kibble seems to fall out fairly easily, as do the oval-shaped biscuits, thus rewarding the dog instantaneously for checking out the chewtoys. The bone-shaped biscuits fall out after a while, rewarding the dog for worrying at the chewtoy. But the triangular biscuits never come out. They remain inside the Kong as lures, maintaining the dog's fascination with its chewtoy. To further focus the dog's interest, I always make sure to flavor the triangular biscuits by rubbing them with a little cheese or freeze-dried liver.

If stuffed chewtoys are reserved especially for times the dog is confined, the puppy-dog will soon learn to enjoy quiet moments in her doggy den and she will quickly develop a chewtoy habit—a good habit! This is a simple *passive training* process; all the owner has to do is set up the situation and the dog all but trains herself—easy and effective. Even when the dog is given run of the house, her first inclination will be to indulge her rewarding chewtoy habit rather than destroying less-attractive household articles, such as curtains, carpets, chairs and compact disks. Similarly, a chewtoy chewer will be less inclined to scratch and chew herself excessively. Also, if the dog busies herself as a recreational chewer, she will be less inclined to develop into a recreational barker or digger when left at home alone.

Stuff a number of chewtoys whenever the dog is left confined and remove the extra-special-tasting treats when you return. Your dog will now amuse himself with his chew-toys before falling asleep and then resume playing with his chewtoys when he expects you to return. Since most owner-absent misbehavior happens right after you leave and right before your expected return, your puppydog will now be conveniently preoccupied with his chewtoys at these times.

Come and Sit

Most puppies will happily approach virtually anyone, whether called or not; that is, until they collide with

To teach come, call your dog, open your arms as a welcoming signal, wave a toy or a treat and praise for every step in your direction.

adolescence and develop other more important doggy interests, such as sniffing a multiplicity of exquisite odors on the grass. Your mission, Mr. and/or Ms. Owner, is to teach and reward the pup for coming reliably, willingly and happily when called—and you have just three months to get it done. Unless adequately reinforced, your puppy's tendency to approach people will self-destruct by adolescence.

Call your dog ("Fido, come!"), open your arms (and maybe squat down) as a welcoming signal, waggle a treat or toy as a lure, and reward the puppydog when he comes running. Do not wait to praise the dog until he reaches you—he may come 95 percent of the way and then run off after some distraction. Instead, praise the dog's *first* step towards you and continue praising enthusiastically for *every* step he takes in your direction.

When the rapidly approaching puppy dog is three lengths away from impact, instruct him to sit ("Fido, sit!") and hold the lure in front of you in an outstretched hand to prevent him from hitting you midchest and knocking you flat on your back! As Fido decelerates to nose the lure, move the treat upwards and backwards just over his muzzle with an upwards motion of your extended arm (palm-upwards). As the dog looks up to follow the lure, he will sit down (if he jumps up, you are holding the lure too high). Praise the dog for sitting. Move backwards and call him again. Repeat this many times over, always praising when Fido comes and sits; on occasion, reward him.

For the first couple of trials, use a training treat both as a lure to entice the dog to come and sit and as a reward for doing so. Thereafter, try to use different items as lures and rewards. For example, lure the dog with a Kong or Frisbee but reward her with a food treat. Or lure the dog with a food treat but pat her and throw a tennis ball as a reward. After just a few repetitions, dispense with the lures and rewards; the dog will begin to respond willingly to your verbal requests and hand signals just for the prospect of praise from your heart and affection from your hands.

Instruct every family member, friend and visitor how to get the dog to come and sit. Invite people over for a series of pooch parties; do not keep the pup a secret— let other people enjoy this puppy, and let the pup enjoy other people. Puppydog parties are not only fun, they easily attract a lot of people to help *you* train *your* dog. Unless you teach your dog *how* to meet people, that is, to sit for greetings, no doubt the dog will resort to jumping up. Then you and the visitors will get annoyed, and the dog will be punished. This is not fair. *Send out those invitations for puppy parties and teach your dog to be mannerly and socially acceptable.*

Even though your dog quickly masters obedient recalls in the house, his reliability may falter when playing in the back yard or local park. Ironically, it is *the owner* who has unintentionally trained the dog *not* to respond in these instances. By allowing the dog to play and run around and otherwise have a good time, but then to call the dog to put him on leash to take him home, the dog quickly learns playing is fun but training is a drag. Thus, playing in the park becomes a severe distraction, which works against training. Bad news!

Instead, whether playing with the dog off leash or on leash, request him to come at frequent intervals— say, every minute or so. On most occasions, praise and pet the dog for a few seconds while he is sitting, then tell him to go play again. For especially fast recalls, offer a couple of training treats and take the time to praise and pet the dog enthusiastically before releasing him. The dog will learn that coming when called is not necessarily the end of the play session, and neither is it the end of the world; rather, it signals an enjoyable, quality time-out with the owner before resuming play once more. In fact, playing in the park now becomes a very effective life-reward, which works to facilitate training by reinforcing each obedient and timely recall. Good news!

Sit, Down, Stand and Rollover

Teaching the dog a variety of body positions is easy for owner and dog, impressive for spectators and extremely useful for all. Using lure-reward techniques, it is possible to train several positions at once to verbal commands or hand signals (which impress the socks off onlookers).

Sit and *down*—the two control commands—prevent or resolve nearly a hundred behavior problems. For example, if the dog happily and obediently sits or lies down when requested, he cannot jump on visitors, dash out the front door, run around and chase its tail, pester other dogs, harass cats or annoy family, friends or strangers. Additionally, "sit" or "down" are better emergency commands for off-leash control.

It is easier to teach and maintain a reliable sit than maintain a reliable recall. *Sit* is the purest and simplest of commands—either the dog is sitting or he is not. If there is any change of circumstances or potential danger in the park, for example, simply instruct the dog to sit. If he sits, you have a number of options: allow the dog to resume playing when he is safe; walk up and put the dog on leash, or call the dog. The dog will be much more likely to come when called if he has already acknowledged his compliance by sitting. If the dog does not sit in the park—train him to!

Stand and *rollover-stay* are the two positions for examining the dog. Your veterinarian will love you to distraction if you take a little time to teach the dog to stand still and roll over and play possum. Also, your vet bills will be smaller. The rollover-stay is an especially useful command and is really just a variation of the down-stay: whereas the dog lies prone in the traditional down, she lies supine in the rollover-stay.

As with teaching come and sit, the training techniques to teach the dog to assume all other body positions on cue are user-friendly and dog-friendly. Simply give the appropriate request, lure the dog into the desired body position using a training treat or toy and then *praise* (and maybe reward) the dog as soon as he complies. Try not to touch the dog to get him to respond. If you teach the dog by guiding him into position, the dog will quickly learn that rump-pressure means sit, for example, but as yet you still have no control over your dog if he is just six feet away. It will still be necessary to teach the dog to sit on request. So do not make training a time-consuming two-step process; instead, teach the dog to sit to a verbal request or hand signal from the outset. Once the dog sits willingly when requested, by all means use your hands to pet the dog when he does so.

To teach **down** when the dog is already sitting, say "Fido, down!," hold the lure in one hand (palm down) and lower that hand to the floor between the dog's forepaws. As the dog lowers his head to follow the lure, slowly move the lure away from the dog just a fraction (in front of his paws). The dog will lie down as he stretches his nose forward to follow the lure. Praise the dog when he does so. If the dog stands up, you pulled the lure away too far and too quickly.

When teaching the dog to lie down from the standing position, say "down" and lower the lure to the floor as before. Once the dog has lowered his forequarters and assumed a play bow, gently and slowly move the lure *towards* the dog between his forelegs. Praise the dog as soon as his rear end plops down.

After just a couple of trials it will be possible to alternate sits and downs and have the dog energetically perform doggy push-ups. Praise the dog a lot, and after half a dozen or so push-ups reward the dog with a training treat or toy. You will notice the more energetically you move your arm—upwards (palm up) to get the dog to sit, and downwards (palm down) to get the dog to lie down—the more energetically the dog responds to your requests. Now try training the dog in silence and you will notice he has also learned to respond to hand signals. Yeah! Not too shabby for the first session.

To teach **stand** from the sitting position, say "Fido, stand," slowly move the lure half a dog-length away from the dog's nose, keeping it at nose level, and praise the dog as he stands to follow the lure. As soon

Using a food lure to teach sit, down and stand. 1) "Phoenix, Sit." 2) Hand palm upwards, move lure up and back over dog's muzzle. 3) "Good sit, Phoenix!" 4) "Phoenix, down." 5) Hand palm downwards, move lure down to lie between dog's forepaws. 6) "Phoenix, off. Good down, Phoenix!" 7) "Phoenix sit!" 8) Palm upwards, move lure up and back, keeping it close to dog's muzzle. 9) "Good sit, Phoenix!"

10) "Phoenix, stand!" 11) Move lure away from dog at nose height, then lower it a tad. 12) "Phoenix, off! Good stand, Phoenix!" 13) "Phoenix, down!" 14) Hand palm downwards, move lure down to lie between dog's forepaws. 15) "Phoenix, off! Good down-stay, Phoenix!" 16) "Phoenix, stand!" 17) Move lure away from dog's muzzle up to nose height. 18) "Phoenix, off! Good stand-stay, Phoenix. Now we'll make the vet and groomer happy!"

as the dog stands, lower the lure to just beneath the dog's chin to entice him to look down; otherwise he will stand and then sit immediately. To prompt the dog to stand from the down position, move the lure half a dog-length upwards and away from the dog, holding the lure at standing nose height from the floor.

Teaching *rollover* is best started from the down position, with the dog lying on one side, or at least with both hind legs stretched out on the same side. Say "Fido, bang!" and move the lure backwards and alongside the dog's muzzle to its elbow (on the side of its outstretched hind legs). Once the dog looks to the side and backwards, very slowly move the lure upwards to the dog's shoulder and backbone. Tickling the dog in the goolies (groin area) often invokes a reflex-raising of the hind leg as an appeasement gesture, which facilitates the tendency to roll over. If you move the lure too quickly and the dog jumps into the standing position, have patience and start again. As soon as the dog rolls onto its back, keep the lure stationary and mesmerize the dog with a relaxing tummy rub.

To teach *rollover-stay* when the dog is standing or moving, say "Fido, bang!" and give the appropriate hand signal (with index finger pointed and thumb cocked in true Sam Spade fashion), then in one fluid movement lure him to first lie down and then rollover-stay as above.

Teaching the dog to *stay* in each of the above four positions becomes a piece of cake after first teaching the dog not to worry at the toy or treat training lure. This is best accomplished by hand feeding dinner kibble. Hold a piece of kibble firmly in your hand and softly instruct "Off!" Ignore any licking and slobbering *for however long the dog worries at the treat*, but say "Take it!" and offer the kibble *the instant* the dog breaks contact with his muzzle. Repeat this a few times, and then up the ante and insist the dog remove his muzzle for one whole second before offering the kibble. Then progressively refine your criteria and have the dog not touch your hand (or treat) for longer and longer periods on each trial, such as for two seconds, four seconds, then six, ten, fifteen, twenty, thirty seconds and so on. The dog soon learns: (1) worrying at the treat never gets results, whereas (2) noncontact is often rewarded after a variable time lapse.

Teaching *"Off!"* has many useful applications in its own right. Additionally, instructing the dog not to touch a training lure often produces spontaneous and magical stays. Request the dog to stand-stay, for example, and not to touch the lure. At first set your sights on a short two-second stay before rewarding the dog. (Remember, every long journey begins with a single step.) However, on subsequent trials, gradually and progressively increase the length of stay required to receive a reward. In no time at all your dog will stand calmly for a minute or so.

Relevancy Training

Once you have taught the dog what you expect her to do when requested to come, sit, lie down, stand, rollover and stay, the time is right to teach the dog *why* she should comply with your wishes. The secret is to have many (*many*) extremely short training interludes (two to five seconds each) at numerous (*numerous*) times during the course of the dog's day. Especially work with the dog immediately *before* the dog's good times and *during* the dog's good times. For example, ask your dog to sit and/or lie down each time before opening doors, serving meals, offering treats and tummy rubs; ask the dog to perform a few controlled doggy push-ups before letting her off-leash or throwing a tennis ball; and perhaps request the dog to sit-down-sit-stand-down-stand-rollover before inviting her to cuddle on the couch.

Similarly, request the dog to sit many times during play or on walks, and in no time at all the dog will be only too pleased to follow your instructions because he has learned that a compliant response heralds all sorts of goodies. Basically all you are trying to teach the dog is how to say please: "Please throw the tennis ball. Please may I snuggle on the couch."

Remember, whereas it is important to keep training interludes short, it is equally important to have many short sessions each and every day. The shortest (and most useful) session comprises asking the dog to sit and then go play during a play session. When trained this way, your dog will soon associate training with good times. In fact, the dog may be unable to distinguish between training and good times and, indeed, there should be no distinction. The warped concept that training involves forcing the dog to comply and/or dominating his will is totally at odds with the picture of a truly well-trained dog. In reality, enjoying a game of training with a dog is no different from enjoying a game of backgammon or tennis with a friend; and walking with a dog should be no different from strolling with buddies on the golf course.

Walk by Your Side

Many people attempt to teach a dog to heel by putting him on a leash and physically correcting the dog when he makes mistakes. There are a number of things seriously wrong with this approach, the first being that most people do not want precision heeling; rather, they simply want the dog to follow or walk by their side. Second, when physically restrained during "training," even though the dog may grudgingly mope by your side when "handcuffed" on leash, let's see what happens when he is off leash. History! The dog is in the next county because he never enjoyed walking with you on leash and you have no control over him off leash. So let's just teach the dog off leash from the outset to *want* to walk with us. Third, if the dog has not been trained to heel, it is a trifle hasty to think about punishing the poor dog for making mistakes and breaking heeling rules he didn't even know existed. This is simply not fair! Surely, if the dog had been adequately taught how to heel, he would seldom make mistakes and hence there would be no need to correct the dog. Remember, each mistake and each correction (punishment) advertise the trainer's inadequacy, not the dog's. The dog is not stubborn, he is not stupid and he is not bad. Even if he were, he would still require training, so let's train him properly.

Let's teach the dog to *enjoy* following us and to *want* to walk by our side offleash. Then it will be easier to teach high-precision off-leash heeling patterns if desired. After attaching the leash for safety on outdoor walks, but before going anywhere, it is necessary to teach the dog specifically not to pull. Now it will be much easier to teach on-leash walking and heeling because the dog already wants to walk with you, he is familiar with the desired walking and heeling positions and he knows not to pull.

FOLLOWING

Start by training your dog to follow you. Many puppies will follow if you simply walk away from them and maybe click your fingers or chuckle. Adult dogs may require additional enticement to stimulate them to follow, such as a training lure or, at the very least, a lively trainer. To teach the dog to follow: (1) keep walking and (2) walk away from the dog. If the dog attempts to lead or lag, change pace; slow down if the dog forges too far ahead, but speed up if he lags too far behind. Say "Steady!" or "Easy!" each time before you slow down and "Quickly!" or "Hustle!" each time before you speed up, and the dog will learn to change pace on cue. If the dog lags or leads too far, or if he wanders right or left, simply walk quickly in the opposite direction and maybe even run away from the dog and hide.

Practicing is a lot of fun; you can set up a course in your home, yard or park to do this. Indoors, entice the dog to follow upstairs, into a bedroom, into the bathroom, downstairs, around the living room couch, zigzagging between dining room chairs and into the kitchen for dinner. Outdoors, get the dog to follow around park benches, trees, shrubs and along walkways and lines in the grass. (For safety outdoors, it is advisable to attach a long line on the dog, but never exert corrective tension on the line.)

Remember, following has a lot to do with attitude—*your* attitude! Most probably your dog will *not* want to follow Mr. Grumpy Troll with the personality of wilted lettuce. Lighten up—walk with a jaunty step, whistle a happy tune, sing, skip and tell jokes to your dog and he will be right there by your side.

BY YOUR SIDE

It is smart to train the dog to walk close on one side or the other—either side will do, your choice. When walking, jogging or cycling, it is generally bad news to have the dog suddenly cut in front of you. In fact, I train my dogs to walk "By my side" and "Other side"—both very useful instructions. It is possible to position the dog fairly accurately by looking to the appropriate side and clicking your fingers or slapping your thigh on that side. A precise positioning may be attained by holding a training lure, such as a chewtoy, tennis ball, or food treat. Stop and stand still several times throughout the walk, just as you would when window shopping or meeting a friend. Use the lure to make sure the dog slows down and stays close whenever you stop.

When teaching the dog to heel, we generally want her to sit in heel position when we stop. Teach heel

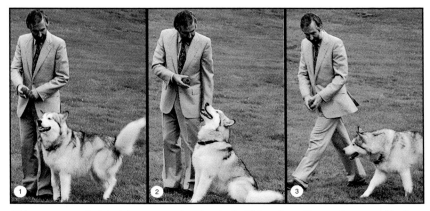

Using a toy to teach sit-heel-sit sequences: 1) "Phoenix, heel!" Standing still, move lure up and back over dog's muzzle…. 2) To position dog sitting in heel position on your left side. 3) "Phoenix, heel!" wagging lure in left hand. Change lure to right hand in preparation for sit signal.

position at the standstill and the dog will learn that the default heel position is sitting by your side (left or right—your choice, unless you wish to compete in obedience trials, in which case the dog must heel on the left).

Several times a day, stand up and call your dog to come and sit in heel position—"Fido, heel!" For example, instruct the dog to come to heel each time there are commercials on TV, or each time you turn a page of a novel, and the dog will get it in a single evening.

Practice straight-line heeling and turns separately. With the dog sitting at heel, teach him to turn in place. After each quarter-turn, half-turn or full turn in place, lure the dog to sit at heel. Now it's time for short straight-line heeling sequences, no more than a few steps at a time. Always think of heeling in terms of Sit-Heel-Sit sequences—start and end with the dog in position and do your best to keep him there when moving. Progressively increase the number of steps in each sequence. When the dog remains close for 20 yards of straight-line heeling, it is time to add a few turns and then sign up for a happy-heeling obedience class to get some advice from the experts.

4) Use hand signal only to lure dog to sit as you stop. Eventually, dog will sit automatically at heel whenever you stop. 5) "Good dog!"

No Pulling on Leash

You can start teaching your dog not to pull on leash anywhere—in front of the television or outdoors—but regardless of location, you must not take a single step with tension in the leash. For a reason known only to dogs, even just a couple of paces of pulling on leash is intrinsically motivating and diabolically rewarding. Instead, attach the leash to the dog's collar, grasp the other end firmly with both hands held close to your chest, and stand still—do not budge an inch. Have somebody watch you with a stopwatch to time your progress, or else you will never believe this will work and so you will not even try the exercise, and your shoulder and the dog's neck will be traumatized for years to come.

Stand still and wait for the dog to stop pulling, and to sit and/or lie down. All dogs stop pulling and sit eventually. Most take only a couple of minutes; the all-time record is 22 $\frac{1}{5}$ minutes. Time how long it takes. Gently praise the dog when he stops pulling, and as soon as he sits, enthusiastically praise the dog and take just one step forwards, then immediately stand still. This single step usually demonstrates the ballistic reinforcing nature of pulling on leash; most dogs explode to the end of the leash, so be prepared for the strain. Stand firm and wait for the dog to sit again. Repeat this half a dozen times and you will probably notice a progressive reduction in the force of the dog's one-step explosions and a radical reduction in the time it takes for the dog to sit each time.

As the dog learns "Sit we go" and "Pull we stop," she will begin to walk forward calmly with each single step and automatically sit when you stop. Now try two steps before you stop. Wooooooo! Scary! When the dog has mastered two steps at a time, try for three. After each success, progressively increase the number of steps in the sequence: try four steps and then six, eight, ten and twenty steps before stopping. Congratulations! You are now walking the dog on leash.

Whenever walking with the dog (off leash or on leash), make sure you stop periodically to practice a few position commands and stays before instructing the dog to "Walk on!" (Remember, you want the dog to be compliant everywhere, not just in the kitchen when his dinner is at hand.) For example, stopping every 25 yards to briefly train the dog amounts to over 200 training interludes within a single three-mile stroll. And each training session is in a different location. You will not believe the improvement within just the first mile of the first walk.

To put it another way, integrating training into a walk offers 200 separate opportunities to use the continuance of the walk as a reward to reinforce the dog's education. Moreover, some training interludes may comprise continuing education for the dog's walking skills: Alternate short periods of the dog walking calmly by your side with periods when the dog is allowed to sniff and investigate the environment. Now sniffing odors on the grass and meeting other dogs become rewards which reinforce the dog's calm and mannerly demeanor. Good Lord! Whatever next? Many enjoyable walks together of course. Happy trails!

THE IMPORTANCE OF TRICKS

Nothing will improve a dog's quality of life better than having a few tricks under its belt. Teaching any trick expands the dog's vocabulary, which facilitates communication and improves the owner's control. Also, specific tricks help prevent and resolve specific behavior problems. For example, by teaching the dog to fetch his toys, the dog learns carrying a toy makes the owner happy and, therefore, will be more likely to chew his toy than other inappropriate items.

More important, teaching tricks prompts owners to lighten up and train with a sunny disposition. Really, tricks should be no different from any other behaviors we put on cue. But they are. When teaching tricks, owners have a much sweeter attitude, which in turn motivates the dog and improves her willingness to comply. The dog feels tricks are a blast, but formal commands are a drag. In fact, tricks are so enjoyable, they may be used as rewards in training by asking the dog to come, sit and down-stay and then rollover for a tummy rub. Go on, try it: Crack a smile and even giggle when the dog promptly and willingly lies down and stays.

Most important, performing tricks prompts onlookers to smile and giggle. Many people are scared of dogs, especially large ones. And nothing can be more off-putting for a dog than to be constantly confronted by strangers who don't like him because of his size or the way he looks. Uneasy people put the dog on edge, causing him to back off and bark, only frightening people all the more. And so a vicious circle develops, with the people's fear fueling the dog's fear *and vice versa.* Instead, tie a pink ribbon to your dog's collar and practice all sorts of tricks on walks and in the park, and you will be pleasantly amazed how it changes people's attitudes toward your friendly dog. The dog's repertoire of tricks is limited only by the trainer's imagination. Below I have described three of my favorites:

SPEAK AND SHUSH

The training sequence involved in teaching a dog to bark on request is no different from that used when training any behavior on cue: request—lure—response—reward. As always, the secret of success lies in finding an effective lure. If the dog always barks at the doorbell, for example, say "Rover, speak!", have an accomplice ring the doorbell, then reward the dog for barking. After a few woofs, ask Rover to "Shush!", waggle a food treat under his nose (to entice him to sniff and thus to shush), praise him when quiet and eventually offer the treat as a reward. Alternate "Speak" and "Shush," progressively increasing the length of shush-time between each barking bout.

PLAYBOW

With the dog standing, say "Bow!" and lower the food lure (palm upwards) to rest between the dog's forepaws. Praise as the dog lowers

her forequarters and sternum to the ground (as when teaching the down), but then lure the dog to stand and offer the treat. On successive trials, gradually increase the length of time the dog is required to remain in the playbow posture in order to gain a food reward. If the dog's rear end collapses into a down, say nothing and offer no reward; simply start over.

BE A BEAR

With the dog sitting backed into a corner to prevent him from toppling over backwards, say "Be a Bear!" With bent paw and palm down, raise a lure upwards and backwards along the top of the dog's muzzle. Praise the dog when he sits up on his haunches and offer the treat as a reward. To prevent the dog from standing on his hind legs, keep the lure closer to the dog's muzzle. On each trial, progressively increase the length of time the dog is required to sit up to receive a food reward. Since lure/reward training is so easy, teach the dog to stand and walk on his hind legs as well!

Teaching "Be a Bear"

chapter 9

Getting
Active
with your Dog

by Bardi McLennan

Once you and your dog have graduated from basic obedience training and are beginning to work together as a team, you can take part in the growing world of dog activities. There are so many fun things to do with your dog! Just remember, people and dogs don't always learn at the same pace, so don't be upset if you (or your dog) need more than two basic training courses before your team becomes operational. Even smart dogs don't go straight to college from kindergarten!

Just as there are events geared to certain types of dogs, so there are ones that are more appealing to certain types of people. In some activities, you give the commands and your dog does the work (upland game hunting is one example), while in others, such as agility, you'll both get a workout. You may want to aim for prestigious titles to add to your dog's name, or you may want nothing more than the sheer enjoyment of being around other people and their dogs. Passive or active, participation has its own rewards.

Consider your dog's physical capabilities when looking into any of the canine activities. It's easy to see that a Basset Hound is not built for the racetrack, nor would a Chihuahua be the breed of choice for pulling a sled. A loyal dog will attempt almost anything you ask him to do, so it is up to you to know your dog's limitations.

All dogs seem to love playing flyball.

A dog must be physically sound in order to compete at any level in athletic activities, and being mentally sound is a definite plus. Advanced age, however, may not be a deterrent. Many dogs still hunt and herd at ten or twelve years of age. It's entirely possible for dogs to be "fit at 50." Take your dog for a checkup, explain to your vet the type of activity you have in mind and be guided by his or her findings.

You needn't be restricted to breed-specific sports if it's only fun you're after. Certain AKC activities are limited to designated breeds; however, as each new trial, test or sport has grown in popularity, so has the variety of breeds encouraged to participate at a fun level.

But don't shortchange your fun, or that of your dog, by thinking only of the basic function of her breed. Once a dog has learned how to learn, she can be taught to do just about anything as long as the size of the dog is right for the job and you both think it is fun and rewarding. In other words, you are a team.

To get involved in any of the activities detailed in this chapter, look for the names and addresses of the organizations that sponsor them in Chapter 13. You can also ask your breeder or a local dog trainer for contacts.

Official American Kennel Club Activities

The following tests and trials are some of the events sanctioned by the AKC and sponsored by various dog clubs. Your dog's expertise will be rewarded with impressive titles. You can participate just for fun, or be competitive and go for those awards.

OBEDIENCE

Training classes begin with pups as young as three months of age in kindergarten puppy training,

You can compete in obedience trials with a well trained dog.

then advance to pre-novice (all exercises on lead) and go on to novice, which is where you'll start off-lead work. In obedience classes dogs learn to sit, stay, heel and come through a variety of exercises. Once you've got the basics down, you can enter obedience trials and work toward earning your dog's first degree, a C.D. (Companion Dog).

The next level is called "Open," in which jumps and retrieves perk up the dog's interest. Passing grades in competition at this level earn a C.D.X. (Companion Dog Excellent). Beyond that lies the goal of the most ambitious—Utility (U.D. and even U.D.X. or OTCh, an Obedience Champion).

AGILITY

All dogs can participate in the latest canine sport to have gained worldwide popularity for its fun and excitement, agility. It began in England as a canine version of horse show-jumping, but because dogs are more agile and able to perform on verbal commands, extra feats were added such as climbing, balancing and racing through tunnels or in and out of weave poles.

Many of the obstacles (regulation or homemade) can be set up in your own backyard. If the agility bug bites, you could end up in international competition!

For starters, your dog should be obedience trained, even though, in the beginning, the lessons may all be taught on lead. Once the dog understands the commands (and you do, too), it's as easy as guiding the dog over a prescribed course, one obstacle at a time. In competition, the race is against the clock, so wear your running shoes! The dog starts with 200 points and the judge deducts for infractions and misadventures along the way.

All dogs seem to love agility and respond to it as if they were being turned loose in a playground paradise. Your dog's enthusiasm will be contagious; agility turns into great fun for dog and owner.

FIELD TRIALS AND HUNTING TESTS

There are field trials and hunting tests for the sporting breeds—retrievers, spaniels and pointing breeds, and for some hounds—Bassets, Beagles and Dachshunds. Field trials are competitive events that test a dog's ability to perform the functions for which she was bred. Hunting tests, which are open to retrievers,

---

TITLES AWARDED BY THE AKC

Conformation: Ch. (Champion)

Obedience: CD (Companion Dog); CDX (Companion Dog Excellent); UD (Utility Dog); UDX (Utility Dog Excellent); OTCh. (Obedience Trial Champion)

Field: JH (Junior Hunter); SH (Senior Hunter); MH (Master Hunter); AFCh. (Amateur Field Champion); FCh. (Field Champion)

Lure Coursing: JC (Junior Courser); SC (Senior Courser)

Herding: HT (Herding Tested); PT (Pre-Trial Tested); HS (Herding Started); HI (Herding Intermediate); HX (Herding Excellent); HCh. (Herding Champion)

Tracking: TD (Tracking Dog); TDX (Tracking Dog Excellent)

Agility: NAD (Novice Agility); OAD (Open Agility); ADX (Agility Excellent); MAX (Master Agility)

Earthdog Tests: JE (Junior Earthdog); SE (Senior Earthdog); ME (Master Earthdog)

Canine Good Citizen: CGC

Combination: DC (Dual Champion—Ch. and Fch.); TC (Triple Champion—Ch., Fch., and OTCh.)

spaniels and pointing breeds only, are noncompetitive and are a means of judging the dog's ability as well as that of the handler.

Hunting is a very large and complex part of canine sports, and if you own one of the breeds that hunts, the events are a great treat for your dog and you. He gets to do what he was bred for, and you get to work with him and watch him do it. You'll be proud of and amazed at what your dog can do.

Fortunately, the AKC publishes a series of booklets on these events, which outline the rules and regulations and include a glossary of the sometimes complicated terms. The AKC also publishes newsletters for field trialers and hunting test enthusiasts. The United Kennel Club (UKC) also has informative materials for the hunter and his dog.

Retrievers and other sporting breeds get to do what they're bred to in hunting tests.

HERDING TESTS AND TRIALS

Herding, like hunting, dates back to the first known uses man made of dogs. The interest in herding today is widespread, and if you own a herding breed, you can join in the activity. Herding dogs are tested for their natural skills to keep a flock of ducks, sheep or cattle together. If your dog shows potential, you can start at the testing level, where your dog can earn a title for showing an inherent herding ability. With training you can advance to the trial level, where your dog should be capable of controlling even difficult livestock in diverse situations.

LURE COURSING

The AKC Tests and Trials for Lure Coursing are open to traditional sighthounds—Greyhounds, Whippets,

Borzoi, Salukis, Afghan Hounds, Ibizan Hounds and Scottish Deerhounds—as well as to Basenjis and Rhodesian Ridgebacks. Hounds are judged on overall ability, follow, speed, agility and endurance. This is possibly the most exciting of the trials for spectators, because the speed and agility of the dogs is awesome to watch as they chase the lure (or "course") in heats of two or three dogs at a time.

TRACKING

Tracking is another activity in which almost any dog can compete because every dog that sniffs the ground when taken outdoors is, in fact, tracking. The hard part comes when the rules as to what, when and where the dog tracks are determined by a person, not the dog! Tracking tests cover a large area of fields, woods and roads. The tracks are laid hours before the dogs go to work on them, and include "tricks" like cross-tracks and sharp turns. If you're interested in search-and-rescue work, this is the place to start.

This tracking dog is hot on the trail.

EARTHDOG TESTS FOR SMALL TERRIERS AND DACHSHUNDS

These tests are open to Australian, Bedlington, Border, Cairn, Dandie Dinmont, Smooth and Wire Fox, Lakeland, Norfolk, Norwich, Scottish, Sealyham, Skye, Welsh and West Highland White Terriers as well as Dachshunds. The dogs need no prior training for this terrier sport. There is a qualifying test on the day of the event, so dog and handler learn the rules on the spot. These tests, or "digs," sometimes end with informal races in the late afternoon.

133

Here are some of the extracurricular obedience and racing activities that are not regulated by the AKC or UKC, but are generally run by clubs or a group of dog fanciers and are often open to all.

Canine Freestyle This activity is something new on the scene and is variously likened to dancing, dressage or ice skating. It is meant to show the athleticism of the dog, but also requires showmanship on the part of the dog's handler. If you and your dog like to ham it up for friends, you might want to look into freestyle.

Lure coursing lets sighthounds do what they do best—run!

Scent Hurdle Racing Scent hurdle racing is purely a fun activity sponsored by obedience clubs with members forming competing teams. The height of the hurdles is based on the size of the shortest dog on the team. On a signal, one team dog is released on each of two side-by-side courses and must clear every hurdle before picking up its own dumbbell from a platform and returning over the jumps to the handler. As each dog returns, the next on that team is sent. Of course, that is what the dogs are supposed to do. When the dogs improvise (going under or around the hurdles, stealing another dog's dumbbell, and so forth), it no doubt frustrates the handlers, but just adds to the fun for everyone else.

Flyball This type of racing is similar, but after negotiating the four hurdles, the dog comes to a flyball box, steps on a lever that releases a tennis ball into the air, catches the ball and returns over the hurdles to the starting point. This game also becomes extremely fun for spectators because the dogs sometimes cheat by catching a ball released by the dog in the next lane. Three titles can be earned—Flyball Dog (F.D.), Flyball Dog Excellent (F.D.X.) and Flyball Dog Champion (Fb.D.Ch.)—all awarded by the North American Flyball Association, Inc.

Dogsledding The name conjures up the Rocky Mountains or the frigid North, but you can find dogsled clubs in such unlikely spots as Maryland, North Carolina and Virginia! Dogsledding is primarily for the Nordic breeds such as the Alaskan Malamutes, Siberian Huskies and Samoyeds, but other breeds can try. There are some practical backyard applications to this sport, too. With parental supervision, almost any strong dog could pull a child's sled.

Coming over the A-frame on an agility course.

These are just some of the many recreational ways you can get to know and understand your multifaceted dog better and have fun doing it.

chapter 10

Your Dog
and your
Family

by Bardi McLennan

Adding a dog automatically increases your family by one, no matter whether you live alone in an apartment or are part of a mother, father and six kids household. The single-person family is fair game for numerous and varied canine misconceptions as to who is dog and who pays the bills, whereas a dog in a houseful of children will consider himself to be just one of the gang, littermates all. One dog and one child may give a dog reason to believe they are both kids or both dogs. Either interpretation requires parental supervision and sometimes speedy intervention.

As soon as one paw goes through the door into your home, Rufus (or Rufina) has to make many adjustments to become a part of your family. Your job is to make him fit in as painlessly as possible. An older dog may have some frame of reference from past experience, but to a 10-week-old puppy, everything is brand new: people, furniture, stairs, when and where people eat, sleep or watch TV, his own place and everyone else's space, smells, sounds, outdoors—everything!

Puppies, and newly acquired dogs of any age, do not need what we think of as "freedom." If you leave a new dog or puppy loose in the house, you will almost certainly return to chaotic destruction and the dog will forever after equate your homecoming with a time of punishment to be dreaded. It is unfair to give your dog what amounts to "freedom to get into trouble." Instead, confine him to a crate for brief periods of your absence (up to three or four hours) and, for the long haul, a workday for example, confine him to one untrashable area with his own toys, a bowl of water and a radio left on (low) in another room.

Lots of pets get along with each other just fine.

For the first few days, when not confined, put Rufus on a long leash tied to your wrist or waist. This umbilical cord method enables the dog to learn all about you from your body language and voice, and to learn by his own actions which things in the house are NO! and which ones are rewarded by "Good dog." House-training will be easier with the pup always by your side. Speaking of which, accidents do happen. That goal of "completely housetrained" takes up to a year, or the length of time it takes the pup to mature.

The All-Adult Family

Most dogs in an adults-only household today are likely to be latchkey pets, with no one home all day but the dog. When you return after a tough day on the job, the dog can and should be your relaxation therapy. But going home can instead be a daily frustration.

Separation anxiety is a very common problem for the dog in a working household. It may begin with whines and barks of loneliness, but it will soon escalate into a frenzied destruction derby. That is why it is so important to set aside the time to teach a dog to relax when left alone in his confined area and to understand that he can trust you to return.

Let the dog get used to your work schedule in easy stages. Confine him to one room and go in and out of that room over and over again. Be casual about it. No physical, voice or eye contact. When the pup no longer even notices your comings and goings, leave the house for varying lengths of time, returning to stay home for a few minutes and gradually increasing the time away. This training can take days, but the dog is learning that you haven't left him forever and that he can trust you.

Any time you leave the dog, but especially during this training period, be casual about your departure. No anxiety-building fond farewells. Just "Bye" and go! Remember the "Good dog" when you return to find everything more or less as you left it.

If things are a mess (or even a disaster) when you return, greet the dog, take him outside to eliminate, and then put him in his crate while you clean up. Rant and rave in the shower! *Do not* punish the dog. You were not there when it happened, and the rule is: Only punish as you catch the dog in the act of wrongdoing. Obviously, it makes sense to get your latchkey puppy when you'll have a week or two to spend on these training essentials.

Family weekend activities should include Rufus whenever possible. Depending on the pup's age, now is the time for a long walk in the park, playtime in the backyard, a hike in the woods. Socializing is as important as health care, good food and physical exercise, so visiting Aunt Emma or Uncle Harry and the next-door neighbor's dog or cat is essential to developing an outgoing, friendly temperament in your pet.

If you are a single adult, socializing Rufus at home and away will prevent him from becoming overly protective of you (or just overly attached) and will also prevent such behavioral problems as dominance or fear of strangers.

Babies

Whether already here or on the way, babies figure larger than life in the eyes of a dog. If the dog is there first, let him in on all your baby preparations in the house. When baby arrives, let Rufus sniff any item of clothing that has been on the baby before Junior comes home. Then let Mom greet the dog first before introducing the new family member. Hold the baby down for the dog to see and sniff, but make sure someone's holding the dog on lead in case of any sudden moves. Don't play keep-away or tease the dog with the baby, which only invites undesirable jumping up.

The dog and the baby are "family," and for starters can be treated almost as equals. Things rapidly change, however, especially when baby takes to creeping around on all fours on the dog's turf or, better yet, has yummy pudding all over her face and hands! That's when a lot of things in the dog's and baby's lives become more separate than equal.

Dogs are perfect confidants.

Toddlers make terrible dog owners, but if you can't avoid the combination, use patient discipline (that is, positive teaching rather than punishment), and use time-outs before you run out of patience.

A dog and a baby (or toddler, or an assertive young child) should never be left alone together. Take the dog with you or confine him. With a baby or youngsters in the house, you'll have plenty of use for that wonderful canine safety device called a crate!

Young Children

Any dog in a house with kids will behave pretty much as the kids do, good or bad. But even good dogs and good children can get into trouble when play becomes rowdy and active.

Teach children how to play nicely with a puppy.

Legs bobbing up and down, shrill voices screeching, a ball hurtling overhead, all add up to exuberant frustration for a dog who's just trying to be part of the gang. In a pack of puppies, any legs or toys being chased would be caught by a set of teeth, and all the pups involved would understand that is how the game is played. Kids do not understand this, nor do parents tolerate it. Bring Rufus indoors before you have reason to regret it. This is time-out, not a punishment.

You can explain the situation to the children and tell them they must play quieter games until the puppy learns not to grab them with his mouth. Unfortunately, you can't explain it that easily to the dog. With adult supervision, they will learn how to play together.

Young children love to tease. Sticking their faces or wiggling their hands or fingers in the dog's face is teasing. To another person it might be just annoying, but it is threatening to a dog. There's another difference: We can make the child stop by an explanation, but the only way a dog can stop it is with a warning growl and then with teeth. Teasing is the major cause of children being bitten by their pets. Treat it seriously.

Older Children

The best age for a child to get a first dog is between the ages of 8 and 12. That's when kids are able to accept some real responsibility for their pet. Even so, take the child's vow of "I will never *ever* forget to feed (brush, walk, etc.) the dog" for what it's worth: a child's good intention at that moment. Most kids today have extra lessons, soccer practice, Little League, ballet, and so forth piled on top of school schedules. There will be many times when Mom will have to come to the dog's rescue. "I walked the dog for you so you can set the table for me" is one way to get around a missed appointment without laying on blame or guilt.

Kids in this age group make excellent obedience trainers because they are into the teaching/learning process themselves and they lack the self-consciousness of adults. Attending a dog show is something the whole family can enjoy, and watching Junior Showmanship may catch the eye of the kids. Older children can begin to get involved in many of the recreational activities that were reviewed in the previous chapter. Some of the agility obstacles, for example, can be set up in the backyard as a family project (with an adult making sure all the equipment is safe and secure for the dog).

Older kids are also beginning to look to the future, and may envision themselves as veterinarians or trainers or show dog handlers or writers of the next Lassie best-seller. Dogs are perfect confidants for these dreams. They won't tell a soul.

Other Pets

Introduce all pets tactfully. In a dog/cat situation, hold the dog, not the cat. Let two dogs meet on neutral turf—a stroll in the park or a walk down the street—with both on loose leads to permit all the normal canine ways of saying hello, including routine sniffing, circling, more sniffing, and so on. Small creatures such as hamsters, chinchillas or mice must be kept safe from their natural predators (dogs and cats).

Festive Family Occasions

Parties are great for people, but not necessarily for puppies. Until all the guests have arrived, put the dog in his crate or in a room where he won't be disturbed. A socialized dog can join the fun later as long as he's not underfoot, annoying guests or into the hors d'oeuvres.

There are a few dangers to consider, too. Doors opening and closing can allow a puppy to slip out unnoticed in the confusion, and you'll be organizing a search party instead of playing host or hostess. Party food and buffet service are not for dogs. Let Rufus party in his crate with a nice big dog biscuit.

At Christmas time, not only are tree decorations dangerous and breakable (and perhaps family heirlooms), but extreme caution should be taken with the lights, cords and outlets for the tree lights and any other festive lighting. Occasionally a dog lifts a leg, ignoring the fact that the tree is indoors. To avoid this, use a canine repellent, made for gardens, on the tree. Or keep him out of the tree room unless supervised. And whatever you do, *don't* invite trouble by hanging his toys on the tree!

Car Travel

Before you plan a vacation by car or RV with Rufus, be sure he enjoys car travel. Nothing spoils a holiday quicker than a carsick dog! Work within the dog's comfort level. Get in the car with the dog in his crate or attached to a canine car safety belt and just sit there until he relaxes. That's all. Next time, get in the car, turn on the engine and go nowhere. Just sit. When that is okay, turn on the engine and go around the block. Now you can go for a ride and include a stop where you get out, leaving the dog for a minute or two.

On a warm day, always park in the shade and leave windows open several inches. And return quickly. It only takes 10 minutes for a car to become an overheated steel death trap.

Motel or Pet Motel?

Not all motels or hotels accept pets, but you have a much better choice today than even a few years ago. To find a dog-friendly lodging, look at *On the Road Again With Man's Best Friend*, a series of directories that detail bed and breakfasts, inns, family resorts and other hotels/motels. Some places require a refundable deposit to cover any damage incurred by the dog. More B&Bs accept pets now, but some restrict the size.

If taking Rufus with you is not feasible, check out boarding kennels in your area. Your veterinarian may offer this service, or recommend a kennel or two he or she is familiar with. Go see the facilities for yourself, ask about exercise, diet, housing, and so on. Or, if you'd rather have Rufus stay home, look into bonded petsitters, many of whom will also bring in the mail and water your plants.

chapter 11

Your Dog
and your
Community

by Bardi McLennan

Step outside your home with your dog and you are no longer just family, you are both part of your community. This is when the phrase "responsible pet ownership" takes on serious implications. For starters, it means you pick up after your dog—not just occasionally, but every time your dog eliminates away from home. That means you have joined the Plastic Baggy Brigade! You always have plastic sandwich bags in your pocket and several in the car. It means you teach your kids how to use them, too. If you think this is "yucky," just imagine what the person (a non-doggy person) who inadvertently steps in the mess thinks!

Your responsibility extends to your neighbors: To their ears (no annoying barking); to their property (their garbage, their lawn, their flower beds, their cat—especially their cat); to their kids (on bikes, at play); to their kids' toys and sports equipment.

There are numerous dog-related laws, ranging from simple dog licensing and leash laws to those holding you liable for any physical injury or property damage done by your dog. These laws are in place to protect everyone in the community, including you and your dog. There are town ordinances and state laws which are by no means the same in all towns or all states. Ignorance of the law won't get you off the hook. The time to find out what the laws are where you live is now.

Be sure your dog's license is current. This is not just a good local ordinance, it can make the difference between finding your lost dog or not.

Dressing your dog up makes him appealing to strangers.

Many states now require proof of rabies vaccination and that the dog has been spayed or neutered before issuing a license. At the same time, keep up the dog's annual immunizations.

Never let your dog run loose in the neighborhood. This will not only keep you on the right side of the leash law, it's the outdoor version of the rule about not giving your dog "freedom to get into trouble."

Good Canine Citizen

Sometimes it's hard for a dog's owner to assess whether or not the dog is sufficiently socialized to be accepted by the community at large. Does Rufus or Rufina display good, controlled behavior in public? The AKC's Canine Good Citizen program is available through many dog organizations. If your dog passes the test, the title "CGC" is earned.

The overall purpose is to turn your dog into a good neighbor and to teach you about your responsibility to your community as a dog owner. Here are the ten things your dog must do willingly:

1. Allow a stranger to handle him or her as a groomer or veterinarian would.
2. Accept a stranger stopping to chat with you.
3. Walk nicely on a loose lead.
4. Walk calmly through a crowd.
5. Sit and be petted by a stranger.
6. Sit and down on command.
7. Stay put when you move away.
8. Casually greet another dog.
9. React confidently to distractions.
10. Accept being tied up in a strange place and left alone for a few minutes.

Schools and Dogs

Schools are getting involved with pet ownership on an educational level. It has been proven that children who are kind to animals are humane in their attitude toward other people as adults.

A dog is a child's best friend, and so children are often primary pet owners, if not the primary caregivers. Unfortunately, they are also the ones most often bitten by dogs. This occurs due to a lack of understanding that pets, no matter how sweet, cuddly and loving, are still animals. Schools, along with parents, dog clubs, dog fanciers and the AKC, are working to change all that with video programs for children not only in grade school, but in the nursery school and pre-kindergarten age group. Teaching youngsters how to be responsible dog owners is important community work. When your dog has a CGC, volunteer to take part in an educational classroom event put on by your dog club.

Boy Scout Merit Badge

A Merit Badge for Dog Care can be earned by any Boy Scout ages 11 to 18. The requirements are not easy, but amount to a complete course in responsible dog care and general ownership. Here are just a few of the things a Scout must do to earn that badge:

Point out ten parts of the dog using the correct names.

Give a report (signed by parent or guardian) on your care of the dog (feeding, food used, housing, exercising, grooming and bathing), plus what has been done to keep the dog healthy.

Explain the right way to obedience train a dog, and demonstrate three comments.

Several of the requirements have to do with health care, including first aid, handling a hurt dog, and the dangers of home treatment for a serious ailment.

The final requirement is to know the local laws and ordinances involving dogs.

There are similar programs for Girl Scouts and 4-H members.

Local Clubs

Local dog clubs are no longer in existence just to put on a yearly dog show. Today, they are apt to be the hub of the community's involvement with pets. Dog clubs conduct educational forums with big-name speakers, stage demonstrations of canine talent in a busy mall and take dogs of various breeds to schools for class-room discussion.

The quickest way to feel accepted as a member in a club is to volunteer your services! Offer to help with something—anything—and watch your popularity (and your interest) grow.

Therapy Dogs

Once your dog has earned that essential CGC and reliably demonstrates a steady, calm temperament, you could look into what therapy dogs are doing in your area.

Therapy dogs go with their owners to visit patients at hospitals or nursing homes, generally remaining on leash but able to coax a pat from a stiffened hand, a smile from a blank face, a few words from sealed lips or a hug from someone in need of love.

Nursing homes cover a wide range of patient care. Some specialize in care of the elderly, some in the treatment of specific illnesses, some in physical therapy. Children's facilities also welcome visits from trained therapy dogs for boosting morale in their pediatric patients. Hospice care for the terminally ill and the at-home care of AIDS patients are other areas where this canine visiting is desperately needed. Therapy dog training comes first.

Your dog can make a difference in lots of lives.

There is a lot more involved than just taking your nice friendly pooch to someone's bedside. Doing therapy dog work involves your own emotional stability as well as that of your dog. But once you have met all the requirements for this work, making the rounds once a week or once a month with your therapy dog is possibly the most rewarding of all community activities.

Disaster Aid

This community service is definitely not for everyone, partly because it is time-consuming. The initial training is rigorous, and there can be no let-up in the continuing workouts, because members are on call 24 hours a day to go wherever they are needed at a moment's notice. But if you think you would like to be able to assist in a disaster, look into search-and-rescue work. The network of search-and-rescue volunteers is worldwide, and all members of the American Rescue Dog Association (ARDA) who are qualified to do this work are volunteers who train and maintain their own dogs.

Physical Aid

Most people are familiar with Seeing Eye dogs, which serve as blind people's eyes, but not with all the other work that dogs are trained to do to assist the disabled. Dogs are also specially trained to pull wheelchairs, carry school books, pick up dropped objects, open and close doors. Some also are ears for the deaf. All these assistance-trained dogs, by the way, are allowed anywhere "No Pet" signs exist (as are therapy dogs when properly identified). Getting started in any of this fascinating work requires a background in dog training and canine behavior, but there are also volunteer jobs ranging from answering the phone to cleaning out kennels to providing a foster home for a puppy. You have only to ask.

Making the rounds with your therapy dog can be very rewarding.

part four

Beyond the Basics

chapter 12

Recommended Reading

Books

ABOUT HEALTH CARE

Ackerman, Lowell. *Guide to Skin and Haircoat Problems in Dogs.* Loveland, Colo.: Alpine Publications, 1994.

Alderton, David. *The Dog Care Manual.* Hauppauge, N.Y.: Barron's Educational Series, Inc., 1986.

American Kennel Club. *American Kennel Club Dog Care and Training.* New York: Howell Book House, 1991.

Bamberger, Michelle, DVM. *Help! The Quick Guide to First Aid for Your Dog.* New York: Howell Book House, 1995.

Carlson, Delbert, DVM, and James Giffin, MD. *Dog Owner's Home Veterinary Handbook.* New York: Howell Book House, 1992.

DeBitetto, James, DVM, and Sarah Hodgson. *You & Your Puppy.* New York: Howell Book House, 1995.

Humphries, Jim, DVM. *Dr. Jim's Animal Clinic for Dogs.* New York: Howell Book House, 1994.

McGinnis, Terri. *The Well Dog Book.* New York: Random House, 1991.

Pitcairn, Richard and Susan. *Natural Health for Dogs.* Emmaus, Pa.: Rodale Press, 1982.

ABOUT DOG SHOWS

Hall, Lynn. *Dog Showing for Beginners.* New York: Howell Book House, 1994.

Nichols, Virginia Tuck. *How to Show Your Own Dog.* Neptune, N. J.: TFH, 1970.

Vanacore, Connie. *Dog Showing, An Owner's Guide.* New York: Howell Book House, 1990.

ABOUT TRAINING

Ammen, Amy. *Training in No Time*. New York: Howell Book House, 1995.

Baer, Ted. *Communicating With Your Dog*. Hauppauge, N.Y.: Barron's Educational Series, Inc., 1989.

Benjamin, Carol Lea. *Dog Problems*. New York: Howell Book House, 1989.

Benjamin, Carol Lea. *Dog Training for Kids*. New York: Howell Book House, 1988.

Benjamin, Carol Lea. *Mother Knows Best*. New York: Howell Book House, 1985.

Benjamin, Carol Lea. *Surviving Your Dog's Adolescence*. New York: Howell Book House, 1993.

Bohnenkamp, Gwen. *Manners for the Modern Dog*. San Francisco: Perfect Paws, 1990.

Dibra, Bashkim. *Dog Training by Bash*. New York: Dell, 1992.

Dunbar, Ian, PhD, MRCVS. *Dr. Dunbar's Good Little Dog Book*, James & Kenneth Publishers, 2140 Shattuck Ave. #2406, Berkeley, Calif. 94704. (510) 658–8588. Order from the publisher.

Dunbar, Ian, PhD, MRCVS. *How to Teach a New Dog Old Tricks*, James & Kenneth Publishers. Order from the publisher; address above.

Dunbar, Ian, PhD, MRCVS, and Gwen Bohnenkamp. Booklets on *Preventing Aggression; Housetraining; Chewing; Digging; Barking; Socialization; Fearfulness; and Fighting*, James & Kenneth Publishers. Order from the publisher; address above.

Evans, Job Michael. *People, Pooches and Problems*. New York: Howell Book House, 1991.

Kilcommons, Brian and Sarah Wilson. *Good Owners, Great Dogs*. New York: Warner Books, 1992.

McMains, Joel M. *Dog Logic—Companion Obedience*. New York: Howell Book House, 1992.

Rutherford, Clarice and David H. Neil, MRCVS. *How to Raise a Puppy You Can Live With*. Loveland, Colo.: Alpine Publications, 1982.

Volhard, Jack and Melissa Bartlett. *What All Good Dogs Should Know: The Sensible Way to Train*. New York: Howell Book House, 1991.

ABOUT BREEDING

Harris, Beth J. Finder. *Breeding a Litter, The Complete Book of Prenatal and Postnatal Care*. New York: Howell Book House, 1983.

Holst, Phyllis, DVM. *Canine Reproduction*. Loveland, Colo.: Alpine Publications, 1985.

Walkowicz, Chris and Bonnie Wilcox, DVM. *Successful Dog Breeding, The Complete Handbook of Canine Midwifery*. New York: Howell Book House, 1994.

About Activities

American Rescue Dog Association. *Search and Rescue Dogs*. New York: Howell Book House, 1991.

Barwig, Susan and Stewart Hilliard. *Schutzhund*. New York: Howell Book House, 1991.

Beaman, Arthur S. *Lure Coursing*. New York: Howell Book House, 1994.

Daniels, Julie. *Enjoying Dog Agility—From Backyard to Competition*. New York: Doral Publishing, 1990.

Davis, Kathy Diamond. *Therapy Dogs*. New York: Howell Book House, 1992.

Gallup, Davis Anne. *Running With Man's Best Friend*. Loveland, Colo.: Alpine Publications, 1986.

Habgood, Dawn and Robert. *On the Road Again With Man's Best Friend*. New England, Mid-Atlantic, West Coast and Southeast editions. Selective guides to area bed and breakfasts, inns, hotels and resorts that welcome guests and their dogs. New York: Howell Book House, 1995.

Holland, Vergil S. *Herding Dogs*. New York: Howell Book House, 1994.

LaBelle, Charlene G. *Backpacking With Your Dog*. Loveland, Colo.: Alpine Publications, 1993.

Simmons-Moake, Jane. *Agility Training, The Fun Sport for All Dogs*. New York: Howell Book House, 1991.

Spencer, James B. *Hup! Training Flushing Spaniels the American Way*. New York: Howell Book House, 1992.

Spencer, James B. *Point! Training the All-Seasons Birddog*. New York: Howell Book House, 1995.

Tarrant, Bill. *Training the Hunting Retriever*. New York: Howell Book House, 1991.

Volhard, Jack and Wendy. *The Canine Good Citizen*. New York: Howell Book House, 1994.

General Titles

Haggerty, Captain Arthur J. *How to Get Your Pet Into Show Business*. New York: Howell Book House, 1994.

McLennan, Bardi. *Dogs and Kids, Parenting Tips*. New York: Howell Book House, 1993.

Moran, Patti J. *Pet Sitting for Profit, A Complete Manual for Professional Success*. New York: Howell Book House, 1992.

Scalisi, Danny and Libby Moses. *When Rover Just Won't Do, Over 2,000 Suggestions for Naming Your Dog.* New York: Howell Book House, 1993.

Sife, Wallace, PhD. *The Loss of a Pet.* New York: Howell Book House, 1993.

Wrede, Barbara J. *Civilizing Your Puppy.* Hauppauge, N.Y.: Barron's Educational Series, 1992.

Magazines

The AKC GAZETTE, The Official Journal for the Sport of Purebred Dogs. American Kennel Club, 51 Madison Ave., New York, NY.

Bloodlines Journal. United Kennel Club, 100 E. Kilgore Rd., Kalamazoo, MI.

Dog Fancy. Fancy Publications, 3 Burroughs, Irvine, CA 92718

Dog World. Maclean Hunter Publishing Corp., 29 N. Wacker Dr., Chicago, IL 60606.

Videos

"SIRIUS Puppy Training," by Ian Dunbar, PhD, MRCVS. James & Kenneth Publishers, 2140 Shattuck Ave. #2406, Berkeley, CA 94704. Order from the publisher.

"Training the Companion Dog," from Dr. Dunbar's British TV Series, James & Kenneth Publishers. (See address above).

The American Kennel Club produces videos on every breed of dog, as well as on hunting tests, field trials and other areas of interest to purebred dog owners. For more information, write to AKC/Video Fulfillment, 5580 Centerview Dr., Suite 200, Raleigh, NC 27606.

chapter 13

Resources

Breed Clubs

Every breed recognized by the American Kennel Club has a national (parent) club. National clubs are a great source of information on your breed. You can get the name of the secretary of the club by contacting:

The American Kennel Club
51 Madison Avenue
New York, NY 10010
(212) 696-8200

There are also numerous all-breed, individual breed, obedience, hunting and other special-interest dog clubs across the country. The American Kennel Club can provide you with a geographical list of clubs to find ones in your area. Contact them at the above address.

Registry Organizations

Registry organizations register purebred dogs. The American Kennel Club is the oldest and largest in this country, and currently recognizes over 130 breeds. The United Kennel Club registers some breeds the AKC doesn't (including the American Pit Bull Terrier and the Miniature Fox Terrier) as well as many of the same breeds. The others included here are for your reference; the AKC can provide you with a list of foreign registries.

American Kennel Club
51 Madison Avenue
New York, NY 10010

United Kennel Club (UKC)
100 E. Kilgore Road
Kalamazoo, MI 49001-5598

American Dog Breeders Assn.
P.O. Box 1771
Salt Lake City, UT 84110
(Registers American Pit Bull Terriers)

Canadian Kennel Club
89 Skyway Avenue
Etobicoke, Ontario
Canada M9W 6R4

National Stock Dog Registry
P.O. Box 402
Butler, IN 46721
(Registers working stock dogs)

Orthopedic Foundation for Animals (OFA)
2300 E. Nifong Blvd.
Columbia, MO 65201-3856
(Hip registry)

Activity Clubs

Write to these organizations for information on the
activities they sponsor.

American Kennel Club
51 Madison Avenue
New York, NY 10010
(Conformation Shows, Obedience Trials, Field
Trials and Hunting Tests, Agility, Canine Good

Citizen, Lure Coursing, Herding, Tracking,
Earthdog Tests, Coonhunting.)

United Kennel Club
100 E. Kilgore Road
Kalamazoo, MI 49001-5598
(Conformation Shows, Obedience Trials, Agility,
Hunting for Various Breeds, Terrier Trials and
more.)

North American Flyball Assn.
1342 Jeff St.
Ypsilanti, MI 48198

International Sled Dog Racing Assn.
P.O. Box 446
Norman, ID 83848-0446

North American Working Dog Assn., Inc.
Southeast Kreisgruppe
P.O. Box 833
Brunswick, GA 31521

Trainers

Association of Pet Dog Trainers
P.O. Box 3734
Salinas, CA 93912
(408) 663–9257

American Dog Trainers' Network
161 West 4th St.
New York, NY 10014
(212) 727–7257

**National Association of Dog Obedience
Instructors**
2286 East Steel Rd.
St. Johns, MI 48879

Associations

American Dog Owners Assn.
1654 Columbia Tpk.
Castleton, NY 12033
(Combats anti-dog legislation)

Delta Society
P.O. Box 1080
Renton, WA 98057-1080
(Promotes the human/animal bond through
pet-assisted therapy and other programs)

Dog Writers Assn. of America (DWAA)
Sally Cooper, Secy.
222 Woodchuck Ln.
Harwinton, CT 06791

National Assn. for Search and Rescue (NASAR)
P.O. Box 3709
Fairfax, VA 22038

Therapy Dogs International
1536 Morris Place
Hillside, NJ 07205